# Manchester United
# Greatest Ever
# Matches

# Manchester United
# Greatest Ever
# Matches

## Steve Bartram
### and
## Adam Marshall

**SIMON &
SCHUSTER**

London · New York · Sydney · Toronto · New Delhi

A CBS COMPANY

First published in Great Britain by Simon & Schuster UK Ltd, 2012
A CBS COMPANY

1 3 5 7 9 10 8 6 4 2

Simon & Schuster UK Ltd
1st Floor
222 Gray's Inn Road
London
WC1X 8HB

www.simonandschuster.co.uk

Simon & Schuster Australia, Sydney
Simon & Schuster India, New Delhi

A CIP catalogue for this book
is available from the British Library.

Hardback ISBN 978-1-47111-057-3

Typeset by M Rules
Printed and bound by CPI Group (UK) Ltd, Croydon, CR0 4YY

# CONTENTS

# ACKNOWLEDGEMENTS

Sincere thanks to Adam Bostock, Nick Coppack, Dan James, Ian Marshall, Craig South, Paul Thomas, Gemma Thompson, James Tuck and James White for their help in collating the initial 100-game 'shortlist', as well as the Manchester United museum staff for their boundless assistance.

For their time, wisdom and animated discussion, we thank the 'other' Old Trafford trinity of Paul Davies, David Meek and Mark Wylie for their integral roles on the judging panel.

Similar gratitude goes out to every single ManUtd.com user who cast their vote for the top ten, as well as each supporter who contributed their fond memories of each game, and sports journalists from over the years who chronicled United in action.

Pictures: John and Matt Peters, Getty Images

# INTRODUCTION

In advance of the 2012-13 season, Manchester United had competed in over 5,200 games. Armed with that perspective, we hope you believe us when we insist that picking the greatest 50 was no easy task.

Such attempts to bring order and rank to a phenomenon of emotion and passion are pretty futile, simply because of their subjectivity. There are no right or wrong answers, because the validity of those answers varies from person to person, yet we have taken steps to safeguard the integrity of this gilded half-century by enlisting help from those who are very much in the know.

An initial shortlist of 100 games (in itself a taxing process) was presented to an expert panel comprising three prominent figures within United circles. The young pup of the litter was Paul Davies, editor of *United Review*, the club's official match-day programme and a veteran of following the Reds across the globe since the early 1990s.

Next came Mark Wylie, curator of the Old Trafford museum and the man charged with telling the full story of United's opulent history on a daily basis. Mark was particularly irked that 1934's invaluable victory at Millwall, which kept the Reds out of Division Three, failed to make the list, but he recovered to take his place on the panel.

Most experienced of all was former *Manchester Evening News* journalist David Meek. The local scribe's first game in the Old Trafford press box was United's FA Cup victory over Sheffield Wednesday in February 1958 – the Reds' first match after the

Munich disaster. David is still an intrinsic part of the club today, ghost-writing Sir Alex Ferguson's programme column.

So the panel, we can safely say, provided an imposing authority on all things United. Fuelled by tea and the promise of sandwiches, they spent hours poring over the shortlist and, promisingly, none raised concerns about glaring omissions. As you come to sift through the 50 games, there will undoubtedly be moments where you pause and wonder to yourself – possibly aloud – how these fools failed to include Norman Whiteside curling United to victory over Everton at Wembley in 1985, 2004's FA Cup semi-final epic against Arsenal, the second leg of the Treble or the victory over Palmeiras that crowned United as kings of planet Earth for the first time.

A case can be made for these games and countless others, but whenever you try to crowbar one in, you find another game set in stone in the half-century. We quarrelled, we bickered, but eventually we concurred. That is not to say we got it right because, as discussed, there is no right or wrong.

Which made for a thankless afternoon for the panel, who were faced with the task of defining a 'great game'. Is it United in top form, pulverising the opposition with a glut of goals? Are more dramatic victories the sweetest, when the full gamut of emotions has been felt during 90 tense minutes? Of course, the magnitude of the match must always be taken into account, with the biggest stage only heightening the drama. Trophies also help sway opinion.

The panel decided that the most crucial factors were if the game itself provided superb entertainment, the occasion was significant, there was a dramatic conclusion and it was vital or at least important in terms of winning trophies. There was also that delightfully intangible quality where a match felt like a 'typical United' game, the *je ne sais quoi* that indelibly embeds a match on one's subconscious without any glaring reason.

Thereafter, the panel carefully deliberated their way through games 50 to 11, putting forward cases and counter-cases for each match to hold a certain position. With a defined top ten United matches established, we filled the trio with sandwiches and put the dectet to the users of ManUtd.com, the club's official website.

There, fans voted in their thousands, scrutinising United's outstanding games and ordering them with an online vote. One game in particular was a nailed-on winner from the outset, but we shan't spoil the surprise. Merely dive in and take the scenic route to the greatest game in the Reds' unique history.

Hopefully, this book will not only evoke fond memories of your time served as a Red, but also provide an enriching education of historical occasions from the long-distant past that thoroughly deserve their place in the Old Trafford pantheon alongside the trophy-laden era overseen by Sir Alex Ferguson.

What we have gleaned in the researching and writing of this book is just how strong an identity and essence United has, marking it out as a club that enthrals and enraptures the footballing public. Ours is a club that has bounced back from a wartime bombing and the cataclysm of Munich, so perhaps it should come as no surprise that drama is so prominent when United take to the field.

For now, relive the games that have assured the Reds of the lofty status as one of the greatest clubs in the world – we hope you enjoy reading the reports as much as we did researching and writing them. In the future, we look forward to witnessing many more contenders for inclusion as the incredible story of Manchester United continues to rumble on.

# 50

## ARSENAL 2
## MANCHESTER UNITED 6

**League Cup fourth round**
**28 November 1990**
**Highbury, London**

# IT'S RAINING GOALS AT HIGHBURY

At a time when 'One-nil to the Arsenal' was an established Highbury soundtrack, United stormed the home of the would-be champions to smash George Graham's unbeaten side for six – as many as the Gunners had conceded in their previous 14 league games.

### WHAT THE PAPERS SAID

'It was Arsenal's first defeat in 17 games this season, their heaviest home loss since the war, and had United taken a fraction more of their chances they would surely have equalled or surpassed Loughborough Town's 8-0 win at Woolwich Arsenal in 1896.'

David Lacey, *Guardian*

The Reds had failed to crack Arsenal's fabled defensive quintet of David Seaman, Lee Dixon, Steve Bould, Tony Adams and Nigel Winterburn five weeks earlier in a ferocious First Division encounter at Old Trafford, when Anders Limpar's winner was overshadowed by a 21-man brawl that cost United a one-point deduction and the Gunners twice as much.

The bad blood that had spilled over at Old Trafford was predicted to simmer once again, only for the leading protagonists – Winterburn and Brian McClair – to pointedly shake hands before kick-off. With the football firmly in focus ahead of any fisticuffs, United set about serving up the sort of devastating attacking play that Alex Ferguson was gradually trying to establish as the Reds' norm.

Just 77 seconds had passed when Clayton Blackmore's 30-yard free-kick rolled inside Seaman's post, and the hosts were rocked as the visitors tore about the field, hassling and harrying their opponents off kilter. Tactically, United had the edge with the unexpected deployment of Danny Wallace as a centre-forward, a move that Adams and Bould were unable to cope with.

The repurposed winger's scurrying industry, allied to the pace of Lee Sharpe, the power of Mark Hughes and Paul Ince and the considered ball-ferrying of McClair and Mike

Phelan, meant United were a constant menace on the counter-attack as Arsenal sought to overturn their deficit.

Just before the break, a quick one-two of sucker punches gave the Reds an unfathomable three-goal lead. First, Hughes slammed in a finish from Wallace's tee-up, before Sharpe pounced on poor control from Dixon and curled an unstoppable right-footed effort into the net, via the underside of Seaman's crossbar.

Suitably lambasted by Graham at half time, Arsenal hit back in the second period and moved to within a goal of parity through Alan Smith's close-range double. As the Gunners pressed, however, United again struck on the break, as Sharpe glanced in Denis Irwin's superb cross with a neat header, before the winger cemented his starlet status by ramming Hughes's through-ball into Seaman's bottom corner.

'Not one of them was with my left foot,' beamed the winger. 'I knew it was my lucky day when I curled a twenty-yard right-footer past David Seaman! To then score a header and another right-footer, all in front of our travelling fans, was the stuff dreams are made of.'

United's travelling fans were pinching themselves when, with nine minutes still remaining, Wallace pounced to tap home the goal his efforts deserved, after Seaman had spilled Hughes's cross. Just past his fourth anniversary at the Old Trafford helm, Ferguson purred: 'They were totally magnificent; it was my biggest victory at United. I saved it for a special occasion!'

## THE TEAMS

**Arsenal:** Seaman; Dixon, Bould, Adams, Winterburn; Thomas, Groves, Davis, Merson, Limpar (Campbell 73); Smith

**Sub not used:** O'Leary

**Goalscorer:** Smith 49, 68

**Manchester United:** Sealey; Irwin, Bruce (Donaghy 73), Pallister, Blackmore; McClair, Ince, Phelan, Sharpe; Hughes, Wallace

**Sub not used:** Webb

**Goalscorers:** Blackmore 2, Hughes 44, Sharpe 44, 75, 78, Wallace 81

ARSENAL 2 – MANCHESTER UNITED 6

# 49 MANCHESTER UNITED 3 LIVERPOOL 0

First Division
24 April 1965
Old Trafford, Manchester

# EE-AYE ADDIO, WE'RE GOING TO WIN THE LEAGUE

## WHAT THE PAPERS SAID

'Manchester United, the classiest team in the country, must surely stride on to the league championship. In this majestic mood, they cannot slip up now. The most notable contribution Liverpool made to this one-sided match was to turn up.'

Ronald Crowther, *Daily Mail*

In an era when this fixture was deemed a Lancashire derby and the banter between the two sets of supporters centred on the simplistic bragging about winning the league or cup, a one-sided affair allowed United to take a giant stride towards the First Division title. Liverpool had the FA Cup final on their minds and a number of injuries to deal with, although Matt Busby was forced to employ left-back Noel Cantwell as centre-forward due to the absence of David Herd.

Although it seems impossible to imagine the Merseysiders ever giving an inch when a league championship was on the line, Paddy Crerand revealed that Bill Shankly could have been forgiven for prioritising the big day out at Wembley and winning the FA Cup for the first time in the club's history. 'In my day, if we weren't winning a trophy then we wanted Liverpool to win it,' he admitted. 'Just because there was a big thing about keeping the title in the north and not letting it go to the south. We all wanted each other to do well.'

Nonetheless, the majority of the 56,000 crowd at Old Trafford anticipated a tense contest, with championship rivals Leeds United also in action and eventually beating Sheffield Wednesday to keep the pressure on in a title race ultimately decided only on goal average.

Certainly, the opening stages were fraught with nerves. Bobby Charlton's slide-rule pass was just too strong for George Best, and John Connelly dragged wide a cross from the lively Northern Irishman. Best was often the focal point for United's attacks, with Denis Law dropping deep to help out in midfield, a policy that would help his team gain the upper hand.

Charlton rocketed a drive against the woodwork, but the breakthrough arrived before half time, with the celebrated Busby Babe involved. Charlton's magnificent pass released Connelly and, when the cross was headed out only to Law, he returned it with interest, as a left-footed shot slammed past Tommy Lawrence.

Crowd favourite Law repeated the dose from close range to give his side some breathing space, bravely converting a Crerand cross at the far post, but it came at a cost. The Scotland striker managed to hobble back to the centre circle after treatment, but took some 15 minutes to reappear with a bandaged right knee after needing more attention to a deep gash.

With United a man short, Liverpool started to make life uncomfortable for the home fans, but Charlton had already tested the sturdiness of the frame of the goal again with another blistering attempt when Crerand's change of pace allowed him to centre for Connelly's simple finish from close range to make the points safe with ten minutes remaining.

Victory in the following game against Arsenal, two days later, while Leeds lost to Birmingham, essentially wrapped up the title – the first since the days of the Busby Babes. The growing influence of Best, Law and Charlton would form the so-called 'United Trinity', with the trio now immortalised in a statue outside the stadium in a fitting tribute to their enduring legacy.

## THE TEAMS

**Manchester United:** P.Dunne; Brennan, A.Dunne; Crerand, Foulkes, Stiles; Connelly, Charlton, Cantwell, Law, Best

**Goalscorers:** Law 40, 57, Connelly 81

**Liverpool:** Lawrence; Lawler, Byrne; Smith, Yeats, Stevenson; Graham, Hunt, Strong, Chisnall, Thompson

# 48 ARSENAL 2
# MANCHESTER UNITED 4

**Premier League**
**1 February 2005**
**Highbury, London**

## WE'LL SEE YOU OUT THERE

'I actually felt like we were already winning before we'd kicked off,' recalls Darren Fletcher, 'because of how Roy acted in the tunnel.'

The Scottish midfielder refers, of course, to Roy Keane's pre-match face-off with Patrick Vieira. For both captains – models of good behaviour, remember – to be squaring up before a ball had been kicked illustrates the flammable peak reached by the United–Arsenal enmity at the time.

### WHAT THE PAPERS SAID

'Some will say, once more, that too much of this game was ugly, but that is to ignore the primitive beauty that existed in this supreme triumph of the will of Sir Alex Ferguson's side. Twice behind, United's defiance was magnificent to behold. For Arsenal, poison might have been sweeter. For United, victory tasted like nectar.'

Oliver Holt, *Daily Mirror*

Forget that both sides were duking it out in the shadow of runaway league leaders Chelsea, already well en route to ratcheting up a record Premier League points total; this was a grudge match, pure and simple, between two sides whose rivalry had developed around silverware, but had now outgrown it.

Their previous league meeting – popularly known as 'pizzagate' for the post-match use of food as projectiles – had set the tone, and Vieira's pre-match heckling of Gary Neville at Highbury sparked Keane into defensive action. The United skipper had to be pulled away from his Arsenal counterpart, and ended his verbal tirade with the now-infamous line: 'We'll see you out there.'

Vieira's quick riposte was to open the scoring after eight minutes, heading in Thierry Henry's corner, but United's response was emphatic. 'There was no way we were losing that game,' continues Fletcher, an emblematic hub of energy in central midfield. 'We were so pumped up.'

It took the Reds just ten minutes to draw level, as Wayne Rooney knocked down Paul Scholes's chipped pass for the onrushing Ryan Giggs.

The Welshman's shot took a deflection off Ashley Cole to wrong-foot Manuel Almunia and nestle in the goal. Somewhat harshly, Giggs would later be stripped of the strike by the Premier League's Dubious Goals Committee.

Dennis Bergkamp subsequently drilled in a clinical low finish to give the Gunners a half-time lead but, within the hour, it had been negated and overturned by a Cristiano Ronaldo brace. Giggs laid on both: firstly releasing the Portuguese speedster to crack home a left-footed finish, then circumnavigating the bewilderingly edgy Almunia before crossing for the simplest of tap-ins.

There had been as many goals as there had bookings – though United led 4-1 in those stakes – and referee Graham Poll was soon required to brandish his red card as Mikael Silvestre inexplicably head-butted Freddie Ljungberg during a break in play. Though the Reds needed to see out the final 21 minutes with only ten men, they actually increased their lead.

A simple act of running down the clock with neat possession play snowballed, as substitute Louis Saha found Scholes who, in turn, knocked a defence-splitting pass into the path of another sub, John O'Shea. The Irishman had been sent on to help shore up United's midfield, but capped his dereliction of duty in the most unforgettable fashion, by clipping home an impish left-footed finish to wrap up a stunning victory and put the Gunners firmly in their place.

## THE TEAMS

**Arsenal:** Almunia; Lauren (Fabregas 83), Campbell (Hoyte 79), Cygan, Cole; Pires, Vieira, Flamini (Reyes 70), Ljungberg; Bergkamp, Henry

**Subs not used:** Lehmann, van Persie

**Goalscorers:** Vieira 8, Bergkamp 36

**Manchester United:** Carroll; G.Neville, Ferdinand, Silvestre, Heinze; Fletcher (O'Shea 61), Keane, Scholes, Ronaldo (Brown 70); Giggs (Saha 77); Rooney

**Subs not used:** Howard, P.Neville

**Goalscorers:** Cole 18 (og), Ronaldo 54, 58, O'Shea 89

# 47

## MANCHESTER UNITED 4
## CHELSEA 0

**FA Cup final**
**14 May 1994**
**Wembley Stadium, London**

# DOUBLE OR QUITS?

So high were the standards set by United's vintage 1993-94 side, that even a slow-burning 4-0 victory in an FA Cup final provoked in-house disparagement. Fresh from ending his initial season at Old Trafford as part of the Reds' first ever Double-winning side, the invariably plain-speaking Roy Keane shrugged: 'We didn't play well in the first half and I don't think we played that well in the second half, but, luckily enough, we managed to score four goals, so it's not bad.'

### WHAT THE PAPERS SAID

'For a long time at Wembley yesterday, it seemed that Manchester United were intent on refusing the embrace of history. But, though this victory was shaped by two penalties within six minutes in the second half, it would be unfair to suggest that they waited for their destiny to force itself upon them. They had, in fact, taken control before they took the lead and, by the end, there was more than a semblance of majesty about their bearing.'

Hugh McIlvanney, *Sunday Times*

The Irishman had a point, as even one of the Reds' greatest teams had to tentatively plot a path around Glenn Hoddle's obdurate Chelsea side before ultimately ploughing through them. An hour had passed with the Blues coming closest to breaking the deadlock when Gavin Peacock, who had scored both winners as Glenn Hoddle's Blues did the league double over the champions, beat Peter Schmeichel with a looping shot that thudded back off the crossbar.

After the break, United went seeking glory and pinned the Londoners back onto the ropes, flooding forward with increasing intensity. Ryan Giggs attempted to weave some magic to unlock the defence, but needed to stretch out a leg to beat Craig Burley to the loose ball after dribbling his way past Steve Clarke. Denis Irwin touched it beyond Eddie Newton and was sent flying by the midfielder for the most obvious of penalties.

Dennis Wise famously tried to bet Eric Cantona he would miss, but, after a lengthy delay, the unflappable Frenchman sent Dmitri Kharine the wrong way in a manner so routine he might as well have been kicking around at a local park. 'Wisey bet him a hundred pounds he would miss,' said Gary Pallister. 'Of course, he scored, but fair play to Dennis – he paid Eric afterwards.'

Six minutes later, David Elleray pointed to the spot again after Frank Sinclair shoulder-barged Andrei Kanchelskis as he latched onto a through ball by Mark Hughes. Chelsea complained the foul took place outside the box and Wise offered Cantona a 'double or quits' wager, but the PFA Player of the Year ignored the fuss to produce an identikit spot-kick. Double it most certainly was, in more ways than one. 'I had no doubt in my mind that he would score,' insisted Steve Bruce.

As the heavens opened, so did the floodgates. United rediscovered the flowing football that had secured eight more points than nearest challengers Blackburn Rovers in the title race. Hughes, excelling against a club he would later play for, pounced on a Sinclair error to steer home another goal that confirmed him as a Wembley specialist – it was his injury-time volley that kept the Reds' FA Cup dream alive at the semi-final stage against Oldham Athletic.

There was one final flourish, Hughes feeding the rampaging Paul Ince who rounded Kharine but unselfishly teed up substitute Brian McClair for a simple tap-in, a gesture indicative of the team spirit that pervaded this fabulous set of players, an intoxicating mixture of skill, strength and speed. It may have taken an hour to reach top gear on this occasion, but it was well worth the wait to land the spoils in such scintillating fashion.

## THE TEAMS

**Manchester United:** Schmeichel; Parker, Bruce, Pallister, Irwin (Sharpe 84); Kanchelskis (McClair 84), Keane, Ince, Giggs; Cantona, Hughes

**Sub not used:** Walsh

**Goalscorers:** Cantona 60 (pen), 66 (pen), Hughes 69, McClair 90

**Chelsea:** Kharine; Clarke, Kjeldbjerg, Johnsen, Sinclair; Wise, Newton, Burley (Hoddle 68), Peacock; Stein (Cascarino 78), Spencer

**Sub not used:** Hitchcock

# 46 MANCHESTER CITY 2
# MANCHESTER UNITED 3

**Premier League**
**7 November 1993**
**Maine Road, Manchester**

## TWO-NIL DOWN, THREE-TWO UP

Having waited 24 years to get back in the European Cup, only to be crushingly eliminated by Galatasaray amid ugly skirmishes, the last place United wanted to be just four days later was Maine Road.

### WHAT THE PAPERS SAID

'Home supporters, their Galatasaray glee barely contained, were jubilant after 45 minutes. Thereafter, City simply had the life throttled out of them. Horton's team were barely able to thread two passes together, with Ince, Keane and Cantona driving with such an intense authority that City suffered a collective migraine at the back.'
Stephen Bierley, *Guardian*

There, inevitably, Manchester City fans indulged in haughty renditions of 'Gal-a-tas-a-ray' and revelled in the Reds' continental demise. Domestically, United had taken 55 of the previous 60 available Premier League points, rendering laughter at their expense a risky business, but still City taunted.

The home support's boldness was twice galvanised in the first half as Niall Quinn – a perpetual pest to the usually imperious pairing of Steve Bruce and Gary Pallister – headed past an uncharacteristically indecisive Peter Schmeichel to give the Blues a two-goal cushion at the interval.

'I was very concerned that we were two goals down and I thought it was going to be one of those weeks,' admitted Alex Ferguson, post-match. 'But I did think the score at half time was a travesty. I simply told our players that if we put on the pressure and kept on playing the football that we're capable of, it would all come right in the end.'

It did, but the Reds' foothold in the game was established through accident rather than design. Michel Vonk's header back to Blues goalkeeper Tony Coton was woefully short, dropping perfectly into Eric Cantona's path, and while Coton would prevail in one-on-ones with Roy Keane and Andrei Kanchelskis, there was never any question of the Frenchman passing up his opening.

It was away from the City goal,

however, where Cantona posed the most problems. Blues manager Brian Horton's deployment of three central defenders – Vonk, Keith Curle and Alan Kernaghan – had tethered Cantona's influence in the first period. When United's talismanic striker went wandering, however, so did City's control of him.

The introduction of substitute Ryan Giggs also proved key. Benched after a lacklustre display in Istanbul, the 19-year-old needed only a solitary touch – an impeccably timed and weighted swoosh of his left foot – to bisect a packed penalty area and tee up Cantona for a simple back-post tap-in.

Twelve minutes left, and both sides knew what was coming. City retreated deeper and deeper, packing their own area, while United poured forward with no second thought given to taking a hard-earned point back to Old Trafford. Lee Sharpe and Denis Irwin had been terrorising City's rookie right-back, Richard Edghill, all afternoon, and the duo combined to devastating effect to lay on the Reds' winner.

As Edghill tucked up tight to him, Sharpe adroitly flicked the ball through the defender's legs and into the path of Irwin, now with room in which to race. The Republic of Ireland international drilled in a fine cross, which just eluded Mark Hughes, but landed at the rampaging feet of Keane to half-volley home.

Comeback complete, the *Schadenfreude* that had cascaded down from the stands had been firmly rammed back down the throats of United's tormentors. Welcome to hell, Blues.

## THE TEAMS

**Manchester City:** Coton; Edghill, Curle, Kernaghan, Vonk, Phelan; McMahon, Flitcroft, White; Sheron, Quinn

**Subs not used:** Dibble, Griffiths, Lomas

**Goalscorer:** Quinn 21, 32

**Manchester United:** Schmeichel; Parker, Bruce, Pallister, Irwin; Kanchelskis (Giggs 76), Ince, Keane, Sharpe; Cantona, Hughes

**Subs not used:** Sealey, Robson

**Goalscorers:** Cantona 52, 78, Keane 87

**MANCHESTER CITY 2 – MANCHESTER UNITED 3**

# 45 NOTTINGHAM FOREST 1 MANCHESTER UNITED 8

Premier League
6 February 1999
City Ground, Nottingham

## THE ASSASSIN STRIKES

Elfin-featured Ole Gunnar Solskjaer wasn't called the Baby-faced Assassin for nothing. The Norwegian may have disliked the nickname, but the manner in which he shot down an already well-beaten Nottingham Forest proved it was entirely apt.

Former United boss Ron Atkinson did enjoy a couple of good days against his old club, but this was a chastening experience. 'In a nutshell, we were murdered,' he admitted, before dead-panning: 'We gave the fans a nine-goal thriller. We're going to start playing for draws now. Either that or snookers!'

Forest's sole contribution to the scoring was Alan Rogers' left-footed finish to a Jean-Claude Darcheville pass in the sixth minute. By then, the visitors were already ahead thanks to Dwight Yorke, whose first-time effort from a Paul Scholes cross flew past Dave Beasant.

A long pass by Jaap Stam allowed Andy Cole to take the ball around Beasant and swiftly restore United's lead in clinical fashion within 60 seconds, but nobody could have expected the ruthless slaughter that followed after the interval. When Scholes hit the frame of the goal, it proved to be only a temporary reprieve for the Premiership strugglers. Such was the competition for places in the Treble-chasing side that the second half almost became a shoot-out between three of the four strikers vying for a start.

Nottingham-born Cole followed up to net when Yorke's shot was mishandled by Beasant and Yorke was in a similarly prime position to convert when Jesper Blomqvist's dribble led to Jon Olav Hjelde deflecting the ball against his own post.

Solskjaer took over from Yorke in the 71st minute and set about rewriting the record books. 'Four goals as a substitute,' pondered Alex

Ferguson. 'I don't think that's happened before. He's a terrific sub – he picks up the pace of the game straight away.'

The classy David Beckham found pal Gary Neville on the overlap to cross for a Solskjaer tap-in and then put the former Molde marksman in the clear. Beasant saved the attempted chip, but Solskjaer skipped past the stranded keeper and slammed the rebound inside the near post.

With the away fans demanding 'Attack, attack, attack', the Reds obliged, with Scholes superbly driving forward to pick out an unmarked Solskjaer inside the area, who punished the slack marking by volleying home as the ball dropped. There was still time for the goal-hungry Norwegian to add his fourth and complete a Premier League record away win. Nicky Butt's cross was begging to be converted, and Scholes's wild miskick merely diverted it into the path of the grateful Solskjaer, who steadied himself before compounding Beasant's misery.

'I was sitting there thinking: "It's four-one and I'm not coming on today" because Andy and Dwight were on fire,' recalled Solskjaer. 'Then the manager said: "Ole, come and change" and Jim Ryan had a few famous words, like: "We don't need any more

goals so keep the ball, pass it and play nice and simple." Of course, I don't like to do it that way, do I?'

The City Ground clash was also Steve McClaren's first game after being appointed assistant manager and he must've wondered if he'd landed the easiest job imaginable. 'I was just there to watch and I enjoyed it immensely,' he commented. 'It was an excellent performance. I just observed and took notes.' The rest of the football world certainly took note: 1999 was to become Manchester United's year.

## THE TEAMS

**Nottingham Forest:** Beasant; Harkes, Armstrong (Porfirio 73), Palmer, Rogers; Hjelde, Gemmill (Mattson 56), Johnson, Stone; van Hooijdonk, Darcheville (Freedman 26)

**Subs not used:** Bart-Williams, Crossley

**Goalscorer:** Rogers 6

**Manchester United:** Schmeichel; G.Neville, Stam, Johnsen, P.Neville; Beckham, Scholes, Keane (Curtis 71), Blomqvist (Butt 75); Cole, Yorke (Solskjaer 71)

**Subs not used:** van der Gouw, May

**Goalscorers:** Yorke 2, 66, Cole 7, 49, Solskjaer 80, 87, 90, 90+3

# 44 FC BARCELONA 3
# MANCHESTER UNITED 3

**Champions League Group D**
**25 November 1998**
**Camp Nou, Barcelona**

# THE FOOTBALL FIESTA: PART TWO

In a season where United swept the board, they twice met their match in Louis van Gaal's Barcelona. Two sides imbued with goal-getting bloodlust and indifference for the finer arts of defending served up two six-goal thrillers in the space of ten weeks.

While September's Old Trafford draw was an erratic affair affected by questionable refereeing, the sides' rematch at Camp Nou truly was popcorn football. While United cagily ground out a draw in their next and final group-stage game at home to Bayern Munich, a breezy night in

Barcelona was the perfect stage to come out swinging. In their hosts, who needed to win to stay in the hunt for qualification, the Reds had an opponent also inclined to fight it out. 'Matches like this stretch the nerve ends to the limit,' understated Alex Ferguson after the final whistle.

It was van Gaal's side who struck the first blow, inside a minute. Brazilian striker Sonny Anderson's stabbed finish warmed up the home crowd – a comparatively paltry 67,650, well below capacity – and Barça had the Reds on the ropes for much of the opening half hour, but soon the visitors' first attack yielded a damaging sucker punch. Dwight Yorke took Jesper Blomqvist's pass, motored into a yawning gap in the hosts' defence and drilled a low shot inside Ruud Hesp's post.

Defending had been Barça's undoing in the Champions League – conceding six goals and registering only one win in four previous games – and their balsa backline was shattered again shortly after half time by near-telepathic interplay from United's strikers. Andy Cole dummied

Roy Keane's infield ball, allowing it to run to Yorke, whose first-time return pass almost wrong-footed Samuel Okunowo to the point of collapse and gave Cole the simple task of tucking away a finish.

Rivaldo had been quietly pulling the strings in the Barcelona attack all evening, patiently waiting on the edge of the fray. Suddenly, he waded in. United led for just four minutes before the Brazilian curled a free-kick inside Schmeichel's right-hand post, when the Dane – a fortnight after announcing his impending retirement – had moved the other way.

Nevertheless, United retook the lead. After good work from Paul Scholes and Keane, David Beckham arced in a near-post cross at which Yorke hurled himself, contorting to direct his header over the sprawling Hesp.

Yet it would not be enough. As the game oscillated wildly from end to end, Rivaldo controlled Sergi's cross on his chest, sprung into the air and overhead-kicked his side back on terms. And he wasn't done. After bashing a 30-yard shot against the top of the bar, he back-heeled Giovanni through on goal, only to see

his compatriot thwarted as Schmeichel hurtled from his line to brilliantly keep the scores level.

That they remained locked was only down to Hesp's injury-time save from Cole. The Dutchman flung out his right foot to spare his side defeat, but the final whistle still heralded their elimination. United, meanwhile, would fight on, sparring along a path that ultimately led back to Catalonia.

## THE TEAMS

**FC Barcelona:** Hesp; Celades, Okunowo, Reiziger, Sergi; Giovanni, Xavi, Rivaldo; Figo, Anderson, Zenden

**Subs not used:** Arnau, Cuadrado, Roger, Ciric, Mario

**Goalscorers:** Anderson 1, Rivaldo 57, 73

**Manchester United:** Schmeichel; Brown, Stam, G.Neville, Irwin; Beckham (Butt 82), Keane, Scholes, Blomqvist; Cole, Yorke

**Subs not used:** van der Gouw, P.Neville, Solskjaer, Berg, Curtis, Wilson

**Goalscorers:** Yorke 25, 68, Cole 53

# 43

## LIVERPOOL 1
## MANCHESTER UNITED 2

**FA Cup semi-final**
**17 April 1985**
**Maine Road, Manchester**

# THE MAINE EVENT

'It was a match for men,' declared victorious manager Ron Atkinson afterwards. This semi-final replay may have resembled a battlefield at times, but the character displayed by United, after the circumstances surrounding the original tie, was highly commendable. At Goodison Park, the Reds were twice ready to prepare for another Wembley trip, but goals at the end of both normal and extra time forced a second match, this time closer to home at Maine Road.

### WHAT THE PAPERS SAID

'United deserved their delight at seeing soccer justice done and they can be proud of the quality of football which has taken them to their tenth FA Cup final. No one can dispute that the most significant difference between these two teams was one of paramount importance – the art of finishing with goals of blazing splendour.'

Frank McGhee, *Daily Mirror*

On a memorable night, two of the club's most reliable warriors – Bryan Robson and Mark Hughes – scored to overturn a first-half deficit, while Norman Whiteside, who was to net

the winner against Everton in the final, produced an aggressive performance described as 'militant' by esteemed local journalist David Meek.

It was no place for the faint-hearted as United, acknowledging Everton would surely win the title race, knew what this fixture meant to the supporters. Defeat was not an option. In a raucous atmosphere, Phil Neal cleared off the line from Frank Stapleton before Liverpool drew first blood. Steve Nicol collected a Kenny Dalglish pass, beat Arthur Albiston and centred towards John Wark, with Paul McGrath heading into his own net.

The usually unflappable McGrath was rattled and on the deck moments later, with Wark feeding Nicol and a second goal seemed inevitable. However, the Scot poked his shot wastefully wide and it was to prove extremely costly for the Merseysiders.

Beginning the second half with renewed vigour, United levelled soon after the restart. Robson stormed forwards and demanded a return pass from Stapleton before spearing a long-distance drive into the top corner of the net, despite the desperate clawing of Bruce Grobbelaar's outstretched fingertips.

The much-vaunted Mark Lawrenson–Alan Hansen central defensive partnership was again exposed, when Gordon Strachan jinked his way into a position to thread a pass through to Hughes, after Robson robbed Paul Walsh with a challenge that left the forward in a crumpled heap. The young Welshman took aim and made it 25 goals for the season with a low drive inside Grobbelaar's post.

Referee Keith Hackett somehow showed only two yellow cards as the tackles flew in and United had to battle to avoid another Liverpool comeback. Gary Bailey made one dramatic save to push over a lob by Kevin MacDonald, but the team defended valiantly and Joe Fagan's befuddling substitution of Dalglish for defender Gary Gillespie – later rumoured to be the result of a breakdown in communication – only further blunted his side's attack in the absence of the injured Ian Rush.

Hackett ended the tension with the final whistle and a pitch invasion led to Robson being chaired off, not for the first time, by jubilant supporters. 'Liverpool are the team to beat, as they've done it for years,' said United's Captain Marvel. 'There were doubts at the end, considering they did it twice at the weekend, and they say sometimes it comes in threes, but thankfully it didn't.'

Atkinson was rightfully proud of his players, beaming: 'We had to fight for every ball and we did exactly that. I thought we played with more drive throughout. Now we have the opportunity of getting a reward for the blood and tears that the players have sweated. At the end of the day, we beat them with their own power game, which I rate as a great achievement.'

The result meant United were unbeaten in three years against the dominant Anfield outfit and had won seven of the eight FA Cup ties between the clubs. When it came to the crunch in a one-off battle, the Reds just would not yield to their bitterest rivals.

## THE TEAMS

**Liverpool:** Grobbelaar; Neal, Lawrenson, Hansen, Beglin; Nicol, Whelan, MacDonald, Wark; Dalglish (Gillespie 79), Walsh

**Goalscorer:** McGrath 38 (og)

**Manchester United:** Bailey; Gidman, McGrath, Hogg, Albiston; Strachan, Whiteside, Robson, Olsen; Hughes, Stapleton

**Sub not used:** Duxbury

**Goalscorers:** Robson 47, Hughes 59

# 42

## EVERTON 2
## MANCHESTER UNITED 4

**Premier League**
**28 April 2007**
**Goodison Park, Liverpool**

# WE WANT OUR TROPHY BACK

With four Premier League games remaining of a sapping 2006-07 season, United and Jose Mourinho's Chelsea were almost inseparable. The Reds led the champions by three points, an FA Cup final meeting between the pair had been booked, and both clubs went into early Saturday encounters flanked on either side by Champions League semi-finals.

### WHAT THE PAPERS SAID

'Not for the first time, a comeback from Manchester United that bordered on stupefying. Ferguson cavorted as if the title had been won there and then. It probably has. If the Premier League flag ends up flying at Old Trafford for a ninth season, as is likely now, a case of Ferguson's best vintage wine should be sent, chauffeur-driven, to Goodison Park. Everton and kinship had to be thanked.'

Jonathan Northcroft, *Sunday Times*

While Chelsea hosted Bolton Wanderers at Stamford Bridge halfway through a tie with Liverpool, United travelled to Goodison Park with one eye firmly on protecting a slender first-leg advantage against the might of Carlo Ancelotti's AC Milan.

United, bereft of injury victims Gary Neville, Rio Ferdinand, Nemanja Vidic and Darren Fletcher, and with Cristiano Ronaldo fit enough only to start on the bench, began the game in dreadful form, and soon fell behind when Alan Stubbs unleashed a thunderous free-kick which nicked Michael Carrick and arced over the dive of Edwin van der Sar.

Everton, playing with the added motivation of remembering their former hero, Alan Ball, who had died five days earlier, flew into challenges and swarmed all around a United side struggling to keep pace. When Manuel Fernandes doubled the hosts' advantage just after half time with an Exocet into van der Sar's top corner, United's only consolation was that Chelsea were being held to a 2-2 scoreline by Bolton.

Then, from nothing, came everything. Toffees goalkeeper Iain Turner, standing in for ineligible United loanee Tim Howard, dropped a routine Ryan Giggs corner at the feet of John O'Shea, who gleefully rifled home his fourth goal of the season from just five shots.

The ball had barely crossed the line

before Sir Alex Ferguson had bundled
Ronaldo onto the touchline. Moments
after joining the fray, the Portuguese's
powerful header was saved by Turner
but, in the ensuing mêlée, Phil Neville
stabbed the ball into his own net to
haul his former side level.

All the momentum was with the
visitors, but the hosts were hardly
helping themselves. When United
finally took the lead, another Everton
gaffe contributed. Tony Hibbert's ill-
advised pass across his own area was
intercepted and eventually worked to
ex-Toffee Wayne Rooney, who calmly
slotted past Turner before bouncing
over to the euphoric away support.

Their mood was helped by events
at Stamford Bridge. 'Chelsea are
finished,' mouthed Sir Alex to his
players, mimicking a 2-2 scoreline
with his fingers to enhance the point.
United weren't finished, however, as
substitute Chris Eagles latched onto
Rooney's through-ball and, having
survived a nervy stumble, curled home
a sumptuous finish to settle a decisive
afternoon in the Reds' favour. Eight
days later, United were champions,
and the events on Merseyside proved
pivotal – though assistant manager
Carlos Queiroz revealed that the

tendrils of doubt had infiltrated the
away dressing room at Goodison Park.

'Forcing the players to keep the
belief, motivation and concentration
was the key,' admitted the Portuguese.
'At half time there were some signs
here or there that the players stopped
believing, but the second half was a
big lesson in attitude and
determination. At the end, there was
only one team who believed.'

## THE TEAMS

**Everton:** Turner; Hibbert, Yobo,
Stubbs, Lescott; Arteta, Neville,
Carsley (van der Meyde 83),
Fernandes, Osman (McFadden 71);
Vaughan (Beattie 71)

**Subs not used:** Wright, Naysmith

**Goalscorers:** Stubbs 12, Fernandes
50

**Manchester United:** van der Sar;
O'Shea, Brown, Heinze, Evra
(Richardson 56); Solskjaer (Eagles
86), Scholes, Carrick, Giggs; Rooney,
Smith (Ronaldo 63)

**Subs not used:** Kuszczak, Lee

**Goalscorers:** O'Shea 61, P.Neville 68
(og), Rooney 79, Eagles 90

# 41

## NEWCASTLE UNITED 2
## MANCHESTER UNITED 6

**Premier League**
**12 April 2003**
**St James' Park, Newcastle**

## MAGPIES MASSACRED

Much of the pre-match hype in advance of title-chasing United's trip to St James' Park actually surrounded a potential late burst for top spot by third-placed Newcastle, while the Reds' aura had been dimmed by a chastening Champions League defeat at Real Madrid four days earlier.

After the final whistle, Paul Scholes left a stunned St James' Park with the match ball as the Magpies were well and truly blown out of the chase by their heaviest home defeat for 42 years. Only one team on view looked worthy of being crowned champions and so it proved.

### WHAT THE PAPERS SAID

'Manchester United found the perfect hangover cure after having all that heady stuff forced down their throats by Real Madrid earlier in the week. The balm took the form of a Newcastle team so poor and compliant that United could afford to give them a goal start before following that with a spectacular thrashing.'

Colin Malan, *Sunday Telegraph*

'Seven or eight goals would not have been beyond us,' said Scholes.

'We had enough chances. After going a goal down, a point would probably have been acceptable but, once we got back, we couldn't stop scoring. We were a little stung by criticism after the Madrid match, but that's part and parcel of playing for Manchester United.'

The game's first noteworthy act followed the daydreamers' script, as Newcastle moved ahead against the run of play. Craig Bellamy's shot was blocked by Fabien Barthez, but the Frenchman had no chance when Jermaine Jenas rattled in a stupendous drive from long distance, after United had failed to properly clear.

Suitably stung, United had settled the outcome by half time. The Magpies' defence stood appealing in vain for offside when Ole Gunnar Solskjaer twisted to hook home a Ryan Giggs cross to draw the Reds level. Scholes's beautiful one-two with Solskjaer allowed the midfielder to volley emphatically past Shay Given, and the midfielder scored again with another spectacular effort when Wes Brown laid the ball into his path following a run by Giggs. Three goals in six minutes.

'This is as impressive a Manchester

United performance as I can remember,' purred Sky Sports co-commentator Andy Gray. 'It's a joy to watch if you're a neutral.' So too was the long-legged slalom of John O'Shea, which took him past two defenders before he lashed a shot against the underside of the crossbar. Giggs was on hand to plunder a fourth goal from the rebound.

Half time provided respite for the hosts, but the second half did not. Gary Neville crossed to the far post for Scholes to squeeze home his hat-trick and an obvious penalty was awarded by referee Steve Dunn when Titus Bramble resorted to desperate measures to halt Diego Forlan. Ruud van Nistelrooy easily beat Given from the spot to extend a fine record from 12 yards.

Barthez's poor kick gifted a late consolation to Shola Ameobi, who converted Jenas's through-ball, but the Reds nevertheless went into their next game – an all-important trip to Highbury to face title rivals Arsenal – on the crest of a wave.

Sir Alex was certainly unfazed by going anywhere after watching his side's demolition job. 'It's great to get six goals at Newcastle,' he remarked.

'It's such a difficult place to come to and you have to conquer the atmosphere and the fans. The scoreline tells you it is the best performance of the season.'

## THE TEAMS

**Newcastle United:** Given; Hughes, Bramble, Woodgate, Bernard; Solano (Ameobi 66), Dyer, Jenas, Robert (Viana 15 (Lua-Lua 66)); Shearer, Bellamy

**Subs not used:** Harper, Griffin

**Goalscorers:** Jenas 21, Ameobi 89

**Manchester United:** Barthez; O'Shea (G.Neville 49), Ferdinand, Brown (Blanc 65), Silvestre; Solskjaer, Keane, Butt, Giggs (Forlan 45); Scholes, van Nistelrooy

**Subs not used:** Ricardo, P.Neville

**Goalscorers:** Solskjaer 32, Scholes 34, 38, 52, Giggs 44, van Nistelrooy 58 (pen)

# 40 NORTHAMPTON TOWN 2 MANCHESTER UNITED 8

**FA Cup fifth round**
**7 February 1970**
**County Ground, Northampton**

## SIX OF THE BEST

'The closest I got to him was when we shook hands at the end of the game,' smiled Ray Fairfax, the luckless Northampton Town defender tasked with shackling George Best on the day the Ulsterman wrote himself into the United record books.

Having been suspended for four weeks – missing five games – for knocking the ball out of referee Jack Taylor's hands at the end of the Reds' League Cup defeat at Maine Road, Best vented his frustration against the helpless Fourth Division Cobblers by bagging six of United's eight goals in a one-sided FA Cup fifth-round tie.

'Certain members of the press were forthright in proclaiming that he should not be recalled; that I should effectively extend his punishment by leaving him out,' recalled then-manager Wilf McGuinness. 'There was no way I was going to heed their advice. George was the type of character who always wanted to prove something to somebody, and I believe he did that day.'

It took Best 20 minutes to work away the ring rust, after which he broke the deadlock by heading in Brian Kidd's cross. He doubled his tally soon afterwards, nudging Paddy Crerand's measured through-ball past goalkeeper Kim Book and sliding home a finish. Two up at the break, there was no hint of what lay ahead.

Kidd teed up Best to complete his hat-trick at the second attempt soon after the interval, then crossed for United's number 11 to head in a fourth. Those goals flanked Alex Stepney's penalty save from Frank Rankmore, and preceded Kidd momentarily taking the limelight from Best by turning in the Reds' fifth goal.

The sixth, inevitably, came from Best, who converted a simple finish after substitute Francis Burns's raking pass, and Kidd notched his second with a routine tap-in. Dixie McNeil and Frank Large gave the home support a pair of late goals to cheer, but, between them, Best completed his double-treble by shimmying his way past Book and tapping in. The Ulsterman flashed a boyish grin at his grounded foe who, having been tormented all afternoon, enquired: 'Haven't you had enough yet?'

Book later recalled the atmosphere in the home dressing room after the final whistle: 'It was deathly quiet for a while. No one said anything until we climbed into the bath, and one of the lads came out with: "That Bestie's a bit useful, isn't he?"'

But it was nothing personal, according to the man who unleashed Best on the Cobblers. 'I'm firmly convinced that he would have done the same no matter what the standard of opposition,' opined McGuinness.

'Northampton were unlucky to encounter him in that mood, but I don't think even Liverpool would have got off any more lightly. That afternoon, he was burning to put on a show, and the outcome was unforgettable.'

## THE TEAMS

**Northampton Town:** Book; Fairfax, Rankmore, Kiernan, Brookes; Felton, Clarke, Ross; McNeil, Large, Fairbrother

**Sub not used:** Hawkins

**Goalscorers:** McNeil 81, Large 89

**Manchester United:** Stepney; Edwards, Ure, Sadler, Dunne; Sartori, Crerand, Morgan; Best, Charlton (Burns 70), Kidd

**Goalscorers:** Best 20, 29, 49, 61, 66, 85, Kidd 64, 76

# 39

## LEICESTER CITY 1
## MANCHESTER UNITED 3

FA Cup final
25 May 1963
Wembley Stadium, London

# OUTFOXED BY UNITED'S SUPER SCOTS

The Queen presented the FA Cup to captain Noel Cantwell, as United collected a first major trophy since Munich with a regal performance in front of almost 100,000 fans at Wembley. A team rebuilt by Matt Busby over five sapping, arduous years would use this triumph as the springboard for more success. Just as in 1990, winning the FA Cup lifted a side that had remarkably been scrapping it out at the wrong end of the table to aspire to greater glory in the years that followed.

### WHAT THE PAPERS SAID

'For two or more seasons, we have been saying that Manchester United must surely do something soon. Now, at last they have – and with what splendour. The tortures of near-relegation forgotten, they contemptuously brushed Leicester aside in this centenary Cup final with the poise, balance and skill of a team who had been expecting victory from the third round onwards.'

David Miller, *The Times*

If Denis Law was an effervescent force in attack – 'a fiery ball of energy' as one journalist put it – the match was arguably won in midfield, with Paddy Crerand dictating matters in typically exuberant style. The Scotland internationals, expensively acquired for £180,000 in total, ran the show with able support from the likes of Bobby Charlton, Johnny Giles and two-goal David Herd.

'We set our stall out to keep possession as much as possible from the start,' explained skipper Noel Cantwell. 'Even if the chances did not come. Leicester accordingly had to do a lot of chasing – something to avoid at Wembley – and, once we began to use the ball well, our confidence returned.'

The Reds had narrowly avoided relegation and were outsiders on the big day, hence the *Sunday Mirror*'s headline 'Leicester Flop', but the patient approach adopted by shrewd tactician Busby reaped dividends. David Gaskell looked a little nervous in the United goal, but the Foxes seemed overawed as a unit and, after a couple of scares, Busby's team assumed control. On the half-hour mark, Law struck in predatory fashion, swivelling to bury a right-footed drive after being set up by Crerand.

'We played better than for a long time,' said Law. 'There was confidence and rhythm in our teamwork. The lads played exceptionally well but, although it may have looked easy, I personally found it harder than I expected.'

This was the perfect arena for United's arch-poacher to puff out his chest and parade his talents. After exchanging passes with Herd moments later, he rounded Gordon Banks but saw his shot blocked by a combination of Richie Norman and Frank McLintock on the line. Even the best keepers had their fingers scorched by Charlton's thunderbolts and, when Banks could only parry a stinging effort from the left-winger, Herd pounced to double the lead.

Leicester should have ensured a nervous finale when reducing the deficit with ten minutes left, after McLintock thumped the ball into the box at the second attempt and Ken Keyworth dived to head home in spectacular fashion.

Instead, the goal merely served to galvanise United into killing the game off, with Law heading against the woodwork from a Herd pass before

Crerand's dribble past tiring opponents allowed Giles to hang up a cross. Banks spilled it to Herd, who poached his second goal of the final.

'I will always believe that this was the single most important trophy in the history of our great club,' said Bill Foulkes years later. 'We'd been down and out after Munich. No club could recover quickly from the kind of devastation that the air disaster had caused. At the final whistle, the initial feeling was one of relief. I was delighted and so was Matt. We had played the better, more stylish football and deserved to win.'

## THE TEAMS

**Leicester City:** Banks; Sjoberg, Norman; McLintock, King, Appleton; Riley, Cross, Keyworth, Gibson, Stringfellow

**Goalscorer:** Keyworth 80

**Manchester United:** Gaskell; Dunne, Cantwell; Crerand, Foulkes, Setters; Giles, Quixall, Herd, Law, Charlton

**Goalscorers:** Law 30, Herd 57, 85

# 38

# MANCHESTER UNITED 3
# JUVENTUS 2

**Champions League Group B
1 October 1997
Old Trafford, Manchester**

# FERGIE'S FLEDGLINGS COME OF AGE

'We are underdogs, which is unusual but fair enough,' admitted Alex Ferguson, his smile betrayed by the steely glint in his eyes. 'They are at the level we want to reach. That's my ambition.'

## WHAT THE PAPERS SAID

'What style, what passion, what a wonderful performance. There is still a long, long way to go but Manchester United last night earned the right to dream of the European glory they crave. In front of a rapturous Old Trafford they gained a victory to cherish, one forged out of adversity and steeped in character.'

Glenn Moore, *Independent*

The United manager was discussing the ominous prospect of hosting Marcello Lippi's Juventus, back-to-back Champions League finalists and United's group stage opponents for the third time in just over a year. The Reds had lost both previous meetings by a solitary goal, but had never looked so inferior behind such a tight scoreline.

'They were the best continental team I ever faced,' recalls Gary Neville. 'The first time we played them, in the Stadio Delle Alpi, was the only time I remember us not having a single shot in a game. They were the benchmark and they took us to school in those first two meetings.'

The second, settled by Alessandro Del Piero's penalty, inflicted United's second home defeat in Europe and the Italian international took just 24 seconds to break the deadlock in his subsequent return to Old Trafford. Ronny Johnsen, starting in midfield in the absence of Roy Keane, who had snapped his cruciate knee ligaments at Leeds four days earlier, shed possession straight from kick-off. The ball was worked to Del Piero to nonchalantly bypass the onrushing Peter Schmeichel and the hurtling Henning Berg before tapping home.

Though immediately on the back foot, United steadied themselves admirably. Teddy Sheringham had a goal ruled out for offside, then hauled the Reds level before half time. Having struggled to make an impact in his first two months as a United player, the 31-year-old striker marked his watershed moment with a precise header that bounced between Angelo Peruzzi and two defenders on the line.

Juventus's aura of invincibility was shattered. So too was their strategy when, midway through the second period, Didier Deschamps picked up a pair of bookings and was dismissed. Without their water carrier, the dam burst and United poured forward before taking the lead on 69 minutes, as Gary Pallister prodded the ball through a ruck of players to substitute Paul Scholes. In nerveless fashion, the midfielder sauntered past Peruzzi and tucked away a left-footed finish.

Scholes's first-half introduction for Nicky Butt – suffering with blurred vision – had prompted a tactical reshuffle for the Reds, with Ryan Giggs moved out to the left flank from a central role behind Sheringham and Ole Gunnar Solskjaer. Thereafter, United clicked and Giggs was peerless. Having crossed for Sheringham's leveller, the unstoppable Welshman confirmed United's victory in the final minute with a goal of speed and audacity, blasting a finish high inside Peruzzi's near post.

Though Zinedine Zidane curled home a delicious injury-time free-kick, United saw out a famous victory which granted them contender status in Europe's top competition. Even Sir Bobby Charlton, not prone to hyperbole, purred: 'The crowd, the players, the whole event against Juventus was something not to be forgotten. It will rank as one of the great, great nights for United. This must be one of the best, if not the best.'

Manchester United had arrived.

## THE TEAMS

**Manchester United:** Schmeichel; G.Neville, Berg, Pallister, Irwin; Beckham, Johnsen, Butt (Scholes 38); Giggs; Sheringham, Solskjaer (P.Neville 48)

**Subs not used:** van der Gouw, May, McClair, Clegg, Curtis

**Goalscorers:** Sheringham 38, Scholes 69, Giggs 89

**Juventus**: Peruzzi; Birindelli, Ferrara, Montero, Dimas; Pecchia (Iuliano 68), Deschamps, Tacchinardi (Pessotto 19); Zidane; Inzaghi, Del Piero (Amoruso 78)

**Subs not used:** Rampulla, Padovano, Fonseca, Zamboni

**Goalscorers**: Del Piero 1, Zidane 90

# 37 WEST HAM UNITED 1
# MANCHESTER UNITED 6

**First Division**
**6 May 1967**
**Upton Park, London**

## HAMMERED BY THE CHAMPIONS

If ever a league title was won in style, it was in the East End of London in 1967. West Ham's trio of Bobby Moore, Geoff Hurst and Martin Peters had won the World Cup a year earlier, but they were chasing shadows for much of the afternoon as the champions ascended their throne in regal fashion.

### WHAT THE PAPERS SAID

'Hail Manchester United! Matt Busby's magnificents are back where they belong – kings of the English soccer castle. And how devastatingly they reclaimed their throne. Here they proved all their challengers mere pretenders. And with gladiatorial grandeur, Denis Law, Bobby Charlton, George Best, Nobby Stiles and their seven superb team-mates gave the Hammers' best-of-the-season crowd the soccer spectacular they expected.'

Ken Montgomery, *Sunday Mirror*

United's own England heroes, Bobby Charlton and Nobby Stiles, were in fabulous form but there were exemplary performances throughout the team. 'It was the closest I have known to a perfect performance,' said David Sadler. 'Somehow, there was a feeling of total football about it.'

Charlton took less than two minutes to start the rout, while Stiles played with a style that dismissed the theory he was best at the destructive elements of the game. As only Nobby could put it, he said afterwards: 'You know, I haven't been booked since Christmas. It's because I'm wearing my teeth. The referees think I'm smiling at them.'

Matt Busby's champions-elect were quickly out of the traps as Jack Burkett dallied when a Stiles shot was blocked, allowing Charlton to steal possession and blast past rookie goalkeeper Colin Mackleworth. The floodgates were opened with John Aston crossing for Paddy Crerand to bag a simple header, and then Mackleworth dropped a John Aston corner to Bill Foulkes, who accepted the gift.

There were still 80 minutes remaining, but a second title in three years was now a mere formality. George Best added a fourth by expertly beating his marker and finishing a clever Stiles pass with his left foot, but the Reds would slow the game to a walking pace at times, easing over the finishing line and showing off a few party tricks at the same time.

The Hammers had the audacity to pull one back at the start of the second half, when Alex Stepney was unsighted by Sadler and unable to prevent a John Charles effort going under his body. It proved to be only a brief moment of respite for the hosts in front of a post-war record gate at Upton Park.

Goalscorer Charles was guilty of a push on Denis Law from a corner, allowing the Scottish striker to convert the resulting penalty and, after Stepney pulled off a fine stop to thwart Peters, Law rounded things off by crashing into the roof of the net after Mackleworth could only parry another attempt by Best.

A pitch invasion towards the end – 'I decided to go outside right near the tunnel and, when I got there, I found we had four outside-rights,' joked Law – and some unsavoury scenes of violence on the terraces

soured the occasion a little, but Busby was justly able to take the acclaim when celebrating lifting the title in such majestic fashion.

'We played like a great team today,' he said. 'We are a great team and we have a great set of supporters. Ability is no longer enough. Although there is no real substitute for it, you need a combination of ability plus work-rate.'

It was a formula that would allow United to conquer Europe a year later in the same swashbuckling style that had accounted for the best that England had to offer.

## THE TEAMS

**West Ham United:** Mackleworth; Burkett, Charles; Peters, Heffer, Moore; Redknapp, Bennett, Boyce, Hurst, Sissons

**Goalscorer:** Charles 46

**Manchester United:** Stepney; Brennan, Dunne; Crerand, Foulkes, Stiles; Best, Law, Sadler, Charlton, Aston

**Goalscorers:** Charlton 2, Crerand 7, Foulkes 10, Best 25, Law 63 (pen), 79

# 36

# MANCHESTER UNITED 6
# ARSENAL 1

**First Division**
**26 April 1952**
**Old Trafford, Manchester**

## BAND ON THE RUN

Arsenal arrived at Old Trafford in search of a miraculous seven-goal victory to take them above league leaders United on the final day of the 1951-52 season. They took part in a seven-goal epic, but could muster only one of them as the Reds provided a devastating exertion of authority to take the title.

### WHAT THE PAPERS SAID

'Whatever hopes Arsenal had of getting a 7-0 win to beat United on goal average for the championship went hopelessly astray when, with the game only eight minutes old, Rowley settled all disputes by scoring his 28th goal of the season. United were clearly superior, always capable of maintaining ascendancy by a combination of virile and polished football.'

Alf Clarke, *Manchester Evening Chronicle*

Having waited for 41 years to reclaim domestic rule, United savoured the occasion in the knowledge that the Gunners, stricken by injury, were never on course to stage a dramatic late coup. From Jack

Rowley's typically clinical opener after eight minutes, there was no looking back, and the unfamiliarly black-and-white clad visitors were dealt another setback when centre-half Arthur Shaw suffered a fractured wrist. The Gunners had to soldier on with ten men.

By the break, United's coronation was assured. Stan Pearson turned in a deflected effort and Roger Byrne profited from fabulous approach play from the unstoppable Rowley, who continued his fine display into the second half by latching onto Johnny Carey's lofted pass and gently lobbing home his second of the game.

Though Freddie Cox briefly gave the travelling supporters cause for celebration with a close-range finish, his consolation strike merely prompted another late wave of attacks by the hosts. Rowley completed his hat-trick from the penalty spot – becoming the first United player to hit 30 goals in a season – before ensuring he had a hand in all six goals by teeing up Pearson for a last-minute tap-in.

After four decades of waiting – albeit interrupted by the somewhat more consuming matter of two world wars – the time had come to celebrate, and both the club and its supporters were ready, even if they had contrasting ideas over how to do it. The final whistle prompted the frantic ushering onto the field of the Beswick Prize Band, whose attempts to strike up 'See the Conquering Hero Comes' were scuppered amid a swarming pitch invasion.

'The paean, alas ended in a stricken wail, as by strangulation,' observed Donny Davies, of the *Manchester Guardian*, 'and red-faced bandsmen could be seen struggling for their lives to get out of the crowd, holding aloft tubas and trombones, cornets and euphoniums, lest these too should be crushed flat in the press.'

Once the teeming mass of revelry had dispersed, Matt Busby and his players made their way to Manchester Town Hall for a civic reception in which the carousers enjoyed an impromptu piano performance from Johnny Carey. The captain was, fittingly, calling the tune after turning in what one reporter termed 'one of his finest performances – a cameo of soccer skill and charm.'

As Arsenal could vouch, the Reds' hulking skipper embodied Busby's first great United team. The title had returned to Old Trafford, with the foundations re-laid for a winning culture over the coming seasons.

## THE TEAMS

**Manchester United:** Allen; McNulty, Aston; Carey, Chilton, Cockburn; Berry, Downie, Rowley, Pearson, Byrne

**Goalscorers:** Rowley 8, 65, 82 pen, Pearson 40, 89, Byrne 42

**Arsenal:** Swindin; Barnes, Smith; Forbes, Shaw, Mercer; Cox, Goring, Holton, Lewis, Roper

**Goalscorer:** Cox 70

# 35

# NEWCASTLE UNITED 0
# MANCHESTER UNITED 1

**Premier League**
**4 March 1996**
**St James' Park, Newcastle**

# YOU MAKE YOUR OWN LUCK

Popular pre-match expectation denoted that this was the night Newcastle would take a giant step towards their coronation, going seven points clear of United, and Kevin Keegan's cavalier side would validate *Match of the Day* pundit Alan Hansen's theory that the Reds would 'win nothing with kids'. Instead, Eric Cantona punctured the Toon Army's inflated expectation with one swipe of his trusty right foot.

## WHAT THE PAPERS SAID

'Overall, Bruce was Manchester United's heroic figure. Deprived of Pallister's company by a recurrence of a back problem, he enjoyed solid support from Gary Neville but often had to cope with the airborne threat of Ferdinand on his own. And this he did with growing authority.'

David Lacey, *Guardian*

But if Cantona's input was the difference on the scoresheet, Peter Schmeichel was just as much of a match-winner with a remarkable

display of defiance, aided and abetted most notably by veteran defender Steve Bruce, who stood out in the most remarkable of rearguard actions, despite almost being ushered into management at the time.

'It's very much a game of luck,' offered Schmeichel, in his only concession of the evening. 'Les Ferdinand had two shots early on and it could've been two-nil.' The Dane twice saved smartly from the striker and also went full length to keep out Peter Beardsley. It soon became clear he was in one of his moods where it would take something exceptional to beat him.

Philippe Albert's free-kick managed it, but lacked the dip to sidle underneath the crossbar, with Ferdinand spurning a chance from the rebound, before the visitors' inspirational keeper frustrated David Ginola and home debutant Faustino Asprilla. After weathering the first-half storm, United scored against the run of play six minutes into the second half.

Former Magpie Andy Cole passed to Phil Neville on the left and the full-back delivered a cross towards the far post, where Cantona was lurking with intent. The volley wasn't the cleanest of strikes, but it was accurate and skipped past Pavel Srnicek to silence the black-and-white-clad hordes. Cantona, conversely, celebrated with a primal roar towards the heavens.

Newcastle were deflated and, despite more pressure, mustered few clear-cut openings. Ferdinand missed with a header and Schmeichel grasped a loose ball when Rob Lee threatened late on, but this was a disciplined defensive performance from a young team rather than a mere 'smash and grab' raid.

'These kids are very, very special,' insisted Schmeichel. 'It's a great example of the confidence and attitude in the team that, when we lose Gary Pallister, one of our best players, just before the kick-off, we still go out there and beat the top team.'

Alex Ferguson appreciated the psychological blow that would help United go on to achieve the second Double in the club's illustrious history. 'Newcastle had the first half and I couldn't wait until the break,' he admitted. 'But then we imposed ourselves. This team I have at the moment can get better. These boys are growing up together and are creating a team spirit which will help all of them.'

The United manager's prophetic words would prove far closer to the mark than those of Newcastle chairman Sir John Hall. Unflustered despite seeing a 12-point lead whittled down to one, albeit with the North-east side having a game in hand, Hall insisted: 'The future is all ours and we are in a position a year earlier than we expected. We'll be dominating British football for the next ten years.' Less than three months on, United were champions; a feat repeated another five times over the next decade.

## THE TEAMS

**Newcastle United:** Srnicek; Barton, Howey, Albert, Beresford; Ginola, Lee, Batty, Beardsley; Asprilla, Ferdinand

**Subs not used:** Watson, Clark, Gillespie

**Manchester United:** Schmeichel; Irwin, G.Neville, Bruce, P.Neville; Sharpe, Keane, Butt, Giggs; Cantona, Cole

**Subs not used:** May, Scholes, Beckham

**Goalscorer:** Cantona 52

# 34

# MANCHESTER UNITED 2
# TOTTENHAM HOTSPUR 1

**Premier League**
**16 May 1999**
**Old Trafford, Manchester**

## ONE DOWN, TWO TO GO

In mid-May of the greatest season of all, there was still no guarantee that United wouldn't end the campaign empty-handed. The 1998-99 saga had three games remaining, each embellished with the prospect of winning a different competition. First up, the Premier League.

A nip-and-tuck title race between United and reigning champions Arsenal had thrilled a nation, with neither side able to forge ahead tellingly. In their penultimate game, Arsène Wenger's side slipped to a dramatic 1-0 defeat at Leeds, an opening only half-taken by United. The Reds' goalless draw at Blackburn 24 hours later established a one-point lead going into the final day of the season, when Tottenham visited Old Trafford and Arsenal hosted Aston Villa.

'Let them win' read a banner among the visiting Spurs supporters, who made no bones of their desire to see Arsenal vanquished. Les Ferdinand clearly had his own agenda, however, as he made a mockery of United's early dominance with an improvised toe-poke over Peter Schmeichel which looped agonisingly inside the Dane's far post.

By this point, United had already found goalkeeper Ian Walker in fine form. A succession of chances came and went but, just as nerves were taking a firm grip of Old Trafford, David Beckham steadied himself and crashed in a stunning curling effort, via the inside of Walker's right-hand post. Cue bedlam.

Half time came at 1-1, while Arsenal were being held 0-0 by Aston Villa at Highbury. Andy Cole replaced Teddy Sheringham, and the substitute validated his introduction within three minutes with the afternoon's telling contribution: latching onto

Gary Neville's flighted pass and bearing down on Walker.

'I remember it like it was yesterday,' recalls the striker. 'As soon as Nev knocked the ball in, it was a bit further than I expected so I knew I had to bring it down with my first touch but, after that, what happened was instinct. It bounced up and then, out of the corner of my eye, I saw Ian Walker in the half-half position, so I just instinctively tossed a lob up, caught it perfectly on the instep and it just bounced into the back of the net.'

Still United pressed for more, but Walker's goal reverted to leading a charmed life as Cole, Dwight Yorke, Nicky Butt and Paul Scholes all passed up opportunities to stem the flow of nerves. 'We were hanging on to a whole season of hard work,' admitted Alex Ferguson, who greeted the long-awaited final peep of referee Graham Poll's whistle by making straight for his reinstated champions and embracing them all.

'What a season. What a fantastic bunch of lads,' he marvelled over the public address system, before handing over to tenor Russell Watson for a rousing rendition of 'Barcelona'. After all, United's season was far from finished. Even in mid-May, this was just the beginning ...

## THE TEAMS

**Manchester United:** Schmeichel; G.Neville, May, Johnsen, Irwin; Beckham, Scholes (Butt 69), Keane, Giggs (P.Neville 79); Sheringham (Cole 46), Yorke

**Subs not used:** van der Gouw, Solskjaer

**Goalscorers:** Beckham 42, Cole 47

**Tottenham Hotspur:** Walker; Carr, Scales (Young 70), Campbell, Edinburgh; Anderton, Sherwood, Freund, Ginola (Dominguez 9 (Sinton 76)); Iversen, Ferdinand

**Subs not used:** Baardsen, Clemence

**Goalscorer:** Ferdinand 24

# 33 MANCHESTER UNITED 9
# IPSWICH TOWN 0

**Premier League**
**4 March 1995**
**Old Trafford, Manchester**

# FORREST UNDER FIRE

Mirroring the undulating Mexican waves which swept across Old Trafford, United hit the heights before sending records tumbling, as Ipswich Town were overwhelmed in the biggest victory of the Premier League era.

## WHAT THE PAPERS SAID

'Once any team scores more than six, then an element of the surreal impinges. This was United's trip to the moon on gossamer wings. Here was football's triple lock of movement, passing and passion, and the only way Ipswich could have prevented it was to have excavated a trench between them and United immediately after half time.'

Stephen Bierley, *Guardian*

The Reds struck nine goals without reply, and over half of them were pilfered by Andy Cole – at the time routinely known as '£7 million Andy Cole' after his British record move from Newcastle – who devoured chances with ruthless glee. Mark Hughes led the line with fire and brimstone and deserved more than his double. Ryan Giggs and Andrei

Kanchelskis, the latter fresh from demanding a transfer, attacked down the flanks at alarming speed.

Once Roy Keane had ended the Town resistance after a quarter of an hour, from Hughes's pass into his path, the mauling began. Cole slid in to angle a Giggs cross past Forrest soon afterwards and made it 3-0 before the interval by bravely converting the rebound, despite being clobbered by the ageing John Wark, when a trademark Hughes bicycle kick left the bar shuddering.

Ipswich had no answer once Denis Irwin's cross went in off Cole as he challenged for the ball with Frank Yallop. The Reds' collective hunger to get in on the act was all-apparent when Giggs's bold, snaking run led to his team-mates queuing up to get the final touch, Hughes obliging at the far post.

Town goalkeeper Craig Forrest tried in vain to stem the tide when blocking a Giggs shot, only for the ball to loop up for Hughes to nod in his second with no thought for the beleaguered Canadian, whose swing on the crossbar served only to highlight his exasperation. Not that any of this slaughter was his fault. Another save to thwart Brian McClair only allowed Cole to pounce on another rebound with goal-thirsty glee for his fourth.

Even when referee Graham Poll offered some sympathy to the visiting keeper, showing only a yellow card for handball outside the box, Paul Ince took full advantage. After grabbing the ball, the midfielder accepted a quick free-kick from Hughes and chipped into an empty net while Forrest was still busy complaining to the official.

In a rare period of mercy, George Burley's side went a quarter of an hour without further punishment, but United had yet to call off the hunt. With three minutes remaining, Giggs, who in the words of the *Sunday People*, 'takes corners better than Nigel Mansell', saw his flag-kick met by Steve Bruce. The ball had been drawn like a magnet to Cole all afternoon and, despite having a defender at his back, he showed strength and skill in a tight situation to spin and rattle in the ninth.

'It was a once-in-a-lifetime performance,' declared Alex Ferguson. 'We like to think we set high standards and we aim to be perfect, but you don't expect to get it. Today was as near as you could get.

Everyone was absolutely brilliant.'

After the biggest league win in 103 years, few disagreed – particularly goal king Cole. 'I came to Manchester United to play alongside the best and I am starting to realise they are the best,' he beamed. 'I've had hat-tricks before, about ten maybe, but that was my first five. I will treasure that for a long time.'

## THE TEAMS

**Manchester United:** Schmeichel; Keane (Sharpe 46), Bruce (Butt 80), Pallister, Irwin; Kanchelskis, Ince, McClair, Giggs; Hughes, Cole

**Sub not used:** Walsh

**Goalscorers:** Keane 16, Cole 24, 37, 53, 65, 89, Hughes 54, 59, Ince 73

**Ipswich Town:** Forrest; Yallop, Wark, Linighan, Thompson; Palmer, Williams, Sedgley, Slater; Mathie, Chapman (Marshall 64)

**Subs not used:** Mason, Morgan

# 32

## MANCHESTER UNITED 3
## BLACKBURN ROVERS 1

Premier League
3 May 1993
Old Trafford, Manchester

# THE CROWNING GLORY

For the first time in 26 years, the chase was over. Liberated of the weight of pressure and expectation, United could finally celebrate being champions – and Old Trafford partied in style on an unforgettable night of revelry and release.

## WHAT THE PAPERS SAID

'There was not a dry eye in the house, and certainly not a dry throat. By the time Manchester United took a break from the champagne to fulfil their last home fixture of a historic season, the celebrations had reached the maudlin stage, and strong men were blubbing. After a wait of 26 years, the party had been in full swing for some 26 hours when United were persuaded to put down the glasses long enough to beat Blackburn 3-1 before an ecstatic crowd. Blackburn had the temerity to take the lead, but then found themselves swept away on a tide of emotion.'

Joe Lovejoy, *Independent*

The match itself, against Blackburn Rovers, had been rendered inconsequential by second-placed Aston Villa's home defeat to Oldham

Athletic the previous day, a result that crowned the Reds as champions for the first time since 1967. While Alex Ferguson had been amid a round of golf when a stranger told him the news, his players' celebrations had begun as the final whistle sounded at Villa Park.

'There were three or four of us to start with,' recalled captain Steve Bruce, whose house hosted the impromptu bash. 'I think the lads must have been sending smoke signals because, before I knew it, every one of them was there! We had a couple of glasses and a few more glasses and we had a nice time.'

The beautifully timed Bank Holiday Monday had allowed many a title party to spill over into a second day, with thousands of ticketless fans flooding the Old Trafford forecourt and drinking the day away. Those fortunate enough to get inside served up a raucous din hours before kick-off, a hullaballoo barely threatened by Kevin Gallacher's niftily taken opener for the visitors. But somehow they cranked up the volume further when Ryan Giggs curled an unstoppable free-kick into Bobby Mimms's top corner after 22 minutes.

The entire game was conducted in

the surreal circumstance of having no bearing on the atmosphere, but United – with one or two players clearly groggy from the previous night's revelry – still seized control of proceedings and forged ahead just after the hour when Eric Cantona fed Paul Ince to slide a finish under the advancing Mimms.

On a night soaked in romance, there seemed no more logical option than to hand a last-minute free-kick to central defender Gary Pallister. The only outfield player without a goal to his name all season duly cracked a low effort inside Mimms's post to further crank up the volume, which reached a crescendo soon afterwards as both Bruce and Bryan Robson lifted the Premier League trophy together.

Poignantly, the whole party was witnessed by Sir Matt Busby, less than a year before he passed away. Amid the post-match merriment in the home dressing room, the former Reds manager quietly thanked each squad member for bringing the

trophy back to Old Trafford, adding yet another layer of gloss to an evening that will glisten through the ages.

## THE TEAMS

**Manchester United:** Schmeichel; Parker, Bruce, Pallister, Irwin; Sharpe (Robson 46), Ince, McClair (Kanchelskis 81), Giggs; Hughes, Cantona

**Sub not used:** Sealey

**Goalscorers:** Giggs 22, Ince 61, Pallister 90

**Blackburn Rovers:** Mimms; Marker (Cowans 73), Hendry, Moran (Andersson 76), Le Saux; Ripley, Atkins, Sherwood, Wilcox; Gallacher, Newell

**Sub not used:** Talia

**Goalscorer:** Gallacher 8

# 31

## MANCHESTER UNITED 6
## ARSENAL 1

Premier League
25 February 2001
Old Trafford, Manchester

# YORKE THEATRE

After ascending to the pinnacle of club football in his first season at Old Trafford, Dwight Yorke was rarely able to scale the same heights over the remainder of his United career – with the exception of one dazzling, virtuoso outing against Arsenal.

## WHAT THE PAPERS SAID

'Equalling their 6-1 humbling here in 1952, Arsenal were defensively bankrupt, naïve beyond belief at times with the hapless Latvian, Igor Stepanovs, resembling a newly born reindeer running on ice. Although they attacked with genuine promise early on, Arsenal were swept aside by the sheer majesty of United's fast-moving counters and devastating finishes.'

Henry Winter, *Daily Telegraph*

Rarely is a title race decided in February, but when league leaders United obliterated the Gunners, their nearest challengers, to open up a 16-point lead before spring had even sprung, the 2000-01 run-in was a mere formality, instigated by Yorke's sensational display. The Tobagonian striker was aided in part by a hapless Arsenal defence, missing old hands

Lee Dixon, Tony Adams and Martin Keown, and Arsène Wenger was left to lament: 'It was like watching a youth team.'

Yet even the most seasoned backline would have struggled to cope with the cerebral laterality of the Reds' opener after just three minutes. Paul Scholes unexpectedly allowed Gary Neville's pass to run through to Yorke, ran onto the striker's through-ball and crossed back to the Reds' number 19, whose ungainly finish found the net to hint that this was going to be his day.

The Gunners responded with a high-quality move of their own, Robert Pires powering through to tee up Thierry Henry for a typically clinical finish past another Frenchman, Fabien Barthez. Game on? Only for a few minutes. The visitors' defence would see to that.

Roy Keane's simple chip sprung a flimsy offside trap and Yorke opened up his body to pass the ball beyond David Seaman. 'You're back!' yelled Keane at the man of the moment, who was soon exposing Igor Stepanovs again when profiting from a wonderful crossfield pass by David Beckham and stroking in to complete a treble inside 22 minutes.

'I don't think I've played as well as I'd like this season,' the former Aston Villa attacker said afterwards. 'I've had to be patient and wait for my chance and, today, I've taken it.'

Yorke was clearly enjoying himself and turned provider after showing his skills on the left flank, leaving Stepanovs trailing in his wake again. The timing of Keane's run coincided with the release of the pass and the irascible Irishman drilled a fourth past a shell-shocked Seaman to register the goal his personal performance merited.

Some Arsenal fans had already started heading for the exits when Nicky Butt comfortably worked his way past Gilles Grimandi – who tripped himself up – and picked out Ole Gunnar Solskjaer, to sweep in majestically at the near post. The onslaught was halted by the half-time whistle, and the Londoners looked to be avoiding any further punishment when Sir Alex withdrew the outstanding Keane and Yorke with a quarter of an hour remaining.

However, if there was one man all Arsenal fans did not want to see on one of their darkest days, it was ex-Spurs favourite Teddy Sheringham. Desperate to get in on the act, he took over when Solskjaer prepared to pull the trigger in the final minute to add the *coup de grâce*, firing into the net with smug satisfaction.

Ever the hard task-master, Sir Alex stressed: 'We won't be talking about championships because if I started talking about them, then there's the possibility the players might relax and we don't want them to relax.' Try as the manager might to prolong his side's relentless pace, however, the title race was already a procession.

## THE TEAMS

**Manchester United:** Barthez; G.Neville, Brown, Stam, Silvestre; Beckham, Butt, Keane (Chadwick 75), Scholes; Yorke (Sheringham 75), Solskjaer

**Subs not used:** Rachubka, Irwin, P.Neville

**Goalscorers:** Yorke 3, 18, 22, Keane 26, Solskjaer 38, Sheringham 90

**Arsenal:** Seaman; Luzhny, Grimandi, Stepanovs, Cole (Ljungberg 45); Pires, Vieira, Parlour (Vivas 69), Silvinho; Wiltord, Henry

**Subs not used:** Manninger, Bergkamp, Kanu

**Goalscorer:** Henry 16

**MANCHESTER UNITED 6 – ARSENAL 1**

# 30

## MANCHESTER UNITED 2
## LIVERPOOL 1

**FA Cup fourth round**
**24 January 1999**
**Old Trafford, Manchester**

# WHO PUT THE BALL IN
# THE SCOUSERS' NET?

For all the nerve-shredding, clock-defying drama of 11 days in May 1999, arguably the pivotal game of United's Treble triumph came in the Reds' FA Cup fourth-round win over Liverpool. This was the Treble in microcosm: an enthralling battle that tested nerve and faith right to the wire, before consuming frustration submitted to raw elation at the last.

### WHAT THE PAPERS SAID

'I'm convinced that Manchester United have a distinct psychological edge over Liverpool. Deep down, regardless of the admiration they have for Liverpool, United always feel that they'll score against them; and, on the sort of day that other teams would have thrown in the towel and conceded that fate wasn't on their side, they stuck to their belief and had the confidence to grab, not only an equaliser, but a second goal that brought the least likely of victories.'

Mark Lawrenson, *Irish Times*

The game began in horrendous fashion for United. The Scoreboard End, teeming with thousands of Liverpool supporters, was a hub of frenzy after just 155 seconds as Vegard Heggem was allowed to get in a cross from the right flank, and he duly found an unmarked Michael Owen to nod the visitors ahead.

'God almighty, you wouldn't think a five-foot, six-inch striker would score with a header in the first minutes at Old Trafford,' Alex Ferguson later fumed. 'I wasn't too pleased with that.'

The United manager was suitably impressed, however, with his side's reaction. Skipper Roy Keane beat David James with an accurate near-post header, only to see it hit the inside of the post and bounce against former colleague Paul Ince, who nudged it off the line to preserve his side's lead.

Pre-match, the game had been billed as the battle between the Premier League's top strike-forces, and Robbie Fowler almost followed Owen's lead with an audacious right-footed effort which arced just past

Peter Schmeichel's top corner.

Though United struggled to haul their front two of Andy Cole and Dwight Yorke into the game, still the chances came. In the second half, Keane had one effort deflected agonisingly wide of a gaping goal, and another thudded back off the inside of James's post to reinforce the growing belief that this would be Liverpool's first FA Cup win over the Reds for nearly 80 years.

Instead, prophetically, a pair of substitutes did the trick for United. First, with two minutes remaining, Ronny Johnsen, on for Henning Berg, won a contentious free-kick that Liverpool's players protested against vehemently. Rather than shoot, however, David Beckham caught everyone out by crossing for Cole, who nodded across the six-yard box for Yorke to tap home.

'Our players were feeling the injustice instead of focusing on their positions,' lamented Liverpool manager Gerard Houllier. 'It affected their morale.' What followed shattered it.

Jaap Stam's long ball reached Paul Scholes, who dallied long enough to have the ball taken off his toes by the Reds' other substitute, Ole Gunnar Solskjaer. The Norwegian shaped to shoot to the far post, but instead slid it through Jamie Carragher's legs, inside James's near post and into instant hero-status at a rocking Old Trafford.

'The Liverpool win gave us such a buzz,' admitted Stam. 'I have never played in a game like it. It's the first time in my career that I have been losing with two minutes to go, only to score two goals and win.' The Dutchman would have to wait only another four months to sample it again . . .

## THE TEAMS

**Manchester United:** Schmeichel; G.Neville (Solskjaer 81), Berg (Johnsen 81), Stam, Irwin; Beckham, Butt (Scholes 68), Keane, Giggs; Cole, Yorke

**Subs not used:** van der Gouw, P.Neville

**Goalscorers:** Yorke 88, Solskjaer 90

**Liverpool:** James; Heggem, Harkness, Matteo, Carragher, Bjornebye; Redknapp, Ince (McAteer 71), Berger; Owen, Fowler

**Subs not used:** Friedel, Kvarme, McManaman, Leonhardsen

**Goalscorer:** Owen 3

# 29 MANCHESTER UNITED 4
# FC PORTO 0

**Champions League quarter-final, first leg**
**5 March 1997**
**Old Trafford, Manchester**

## PORT IN A STORM

Alex Ferguson opted to attack a Porto side rated by many as dark horses to win the Champions League after cruising through their qualifying group, and the manager's boldness led to one of the most memorable performances at Old Trafford during his extraordinary reign.

### WHAT THE PAPERS SAID

'Old Trafford was not so much a cauldron fit for a cavalry charge as a pressure cooker on high-degree control. Perhaps it was the composure with which United tempered their ambition which caught FC Porto unawares. This was no stampede but a sustained questioning of the blend of European and Brazilian class which had been good enough to win Porto's three previous away games in this season's Champions League.'

Jeff Powell, *Daily Mail*

Deprived of the injured Roy Keane, the United manager gave Ronny Johnsen the huge responsibility of defending in midfield, while Ryan Giggs, David Beckham, Andy Cole, Eric Cantona and Ole Gunnar

Solskjaer displayed their attacking intent. The runaway Portuguese league leaders were overwhelmed as the Reds made a semi-final spot a formality ahead of the second leg.

The crowd's strident backing was rewarded after 22 minutes when Beckham's cross was headed goalwards by Gary Pallister and, when Hilario saved, David May scraped the ball into the net, despite virtually being grounded after challenging for the initial centre. 'Although I was still on the floor, I managed to volley it into the roof of the net,' recalled May. 'It was a great feeling to score the first goal in such an important game. That night was one of the best atmospheres I've experienced at Old Trafford.'

Before too long, dreadful defending gifted a chance to Cantona inside the box and his finish went through Hilario's flimsy defences to put United firmly in the driving seat before the break. The onslaught continued in the second half. Giggs tormented the visiting defence all night, saying afterwards: 'This is probably the best game I've ever played for United', and he notched a deserved goal just past the hour.

Cantona's pass with the outside of

his boot fed Cole on the left and, after
the striker cut inside, he spotted Giggs
tearing past him on the overlap. The
Welshman's near-post finish exposed
Hilario's suspect positioning, but it
was a thrilling illustration of the Reds
in full flow. Cole got in on the act to
round off a fabulous night,
confidently clipping over Hilario after
excellent approach work by Johnsen
and Cantona.

The fact that Johnsen showed his
skill in the build-up, beating two
players, emphasised the desire to
attack running through the entire
side. 'I have played a lot of games in
the Champions League, but I have
never been involved in a performance
as magnificent as that one,'
commented the under-rated
Norwegian.

Ferguson was in no doubt about
the quality of the display, against
highly respected opposition. 'Porto
are a class team,' he asserted. 'On the
evidence of tonight, so are we. To be
honest, this was not a result I had
expected. It is beyond my wildest
dreams. We have had a lot of good

performances in my time, but this is
the most emphatic European
performance I have known in such an
important game.'

## THE TEAMS

**Manchester United:** Schmeichel;
G.Neville, Pallister, May, Irwin;
Beckham, Johnsen, Giggs; Cantona,
Cole, Solskjaer

**Subs not used:** van der Gouw,
P.Neville, Cruyff, Poborsky, McClair

**Goalscorers:** May 22, Cantona 34,
Giggs 61, Cole 80

**FC Porto:** Hilario; Sergio Conceicao,
Jorge Costa, Aloisio, Paulinho
Santos; Edmilson, Barroso, Zahovic,
Joao Costa (Jardel 24), Drulovic;
Artur (Rui Barros 46)

**Subs not used:** Wozniak, Fernando
Mendes, Joao Pinto

# 28 ARSENAL 4 MANCHESTER UNITED 5

**First Division**
**1 February 1958**
**Highbury, London**

## THE BABES' FINAL FLOURISH

Verve, swagger and the unequivocal desire to attack; the hallmarks of Matt Busby's Babes were present in all their glory on the afternoon that English football unwittingly got its final glimpse of a team that would never grow old.

### WHAT THE PAPERS SAID

'Never have I seen Manchester United greater – nor have I seen such superb fighting spirit in an Arsenal team for many seasons. All the 63,000 spectators at Highbury will agree this was a match to remember for a long, long time. United made it look so easy. They used the smash-and-grab tactics of Arsenal in their most glorious days.'

Frank Butler, *News of the World*

Five days on from edging a nine-goal thriller at Highbury, United's breathtaking young team was torn apart by the Munich disaster. Of the eight players claimed by the crash, five started against Arsenal, and they collectively played their part in a pulsating encounter that laid bare all the boyish charm of a side intent on winning in style.

From the first whistle, the Reds made a mockery of the pudding pitch and pouring rain, driving forward and forging ahead after only ten minutes. Duncan Edwards, who would lose the fight against his injuries 15 days after Munich, took aim from 25 yards and sent in a low drive that squirmed under Jack Kelsey. The Gunners' goalkeeper was clearly rocked by his mistake, and United would further benefit from his afternoon's work.

There was, however, no blame attached to Kelsey for the visitors' second goal, shortly after the half-hour, as Bobby Charlton capped a surging run from Albert Scanlon by drilling in a typically blistering effort. When Tommy Taylor bundled home a third on the stroke of half time, United appeared home and hosed.

Instead, a stunning spell of defiance from the hosts put the game back in the balance around the hour mark. The game was meandering along in a settled rhythm until the 58th minute, when David Herd turned in a cross from Vic Groves, sparking a blistering fightback from the Gunners.

The home support were soon in rapture as Jimmy Bloomfield struck a brace just seconds apart, first steering a low finish past Harry Gregg, then charging through the reeling Reds defence and hammering in an unstoppable effort. In the space of four minutes, United's three-goal lead had been obliterated.

Yet, somehow, the Babes merely shrugged off the setback and quickly surged ahead again. Only four further minutes had passed when Dennis Viollet guided Scanlon's cross past Kelsey, who was soon under attention again after Taylor's powerful but stoppable shot found its way into the net.

To their credit, Arsenal mustered another late rally when striker Derek Tapscott made the scoreline 5-4, but this time there would be no collapse from the visitors. The final whistle prompted a standing ovation from both sets of supporters for the heroic teams, unaware that the men from Manchester would never again be seen in action together in England.

Though the tragedy of Munich will remain untouched by time, there can at least be some comfort in knowing that the Babes' final farewell was conducted with a fitting flourish.

## THE TEAMS

**Arsenal:** Kelsey; Charlton, Fotheringham; Evans, Groves, Ward; Bowen, Nutt, Tapscott, Herd, Bloomfield

**Goalscorers:** Herd 58, Bloomfield 60, 61, Tapscott 77

**Manchester United:** Gregg; Foulkes, Byrne; Colman, Jones, Edwards; Morgans, Charlton, Taylor, Viollet, Scanlon

**Goalscorers:** Edwards 10, Charlton 34, Taylor 44, 71, Viollet 65

# 27 ARSENAL 1
# MANCHESTER UNITED 3

**Champions League semi-final, second leg**
**5 May 2009**
**Emirates Stadium, London**

# MEN AGAINST CHILDREN

On a hot summer's night in the capital, the players entered the arena to the sight of Arsenal's fans waving flags and anticipating a glorious occasion at the Emirates Stadium. Gunners boss Arsène Wenger promised a 'memorable performance' in his programme notes. He was right. Within 11 minutes, United fans could book their tickets for Rome for a second successive Champions League final.

## WHAT THE PAPERS SAID

'United had been authoritative in every aspect, even if Cristiano Ronaldo stole the attention with two goals. On this showing, he would be a drastic loss should a move to Real Madrid take place in the close season. If this triumph is any guide, his mind is at least fixed on United's affairs for the time being.'

Kevin McCarra, *Guardian*

When the brilliant Cristiano Ronaldo extended the lead to four goals on aggregate just past the hour, a large number of those expectant home fans vacated their seats. Never one to mince his words, Patrice Evra was clear about the gulf in class between the two teams. 'People say that Arsenal play good football but, as far as we're concerned, we dominated them comfortably. Playing well is not everything in this game. We were eleven men and they were eleven children.'

One of the Gunners' callow youths, Kieran Gibbs, slipped crucially when trying to cut out a Ronaldo cross from the left. Ji-sung Park lost his footing as well, but only after scuffing the ball past Manuel Almunia to live up to his billing as a big-game player and so often the scourge of Arsène Wenger's side.

Three minutes later and a bolt out of the blue from the men in blue stunned the footballing world. Ronaldo won a free-kick and decided to take it on himself, even though he was around 40 yards from goal. Almunia, who had kept Arsenal in the tie in the first leg when limiting the Reds to a solitary John O'Shea goal, appeared to dive under the Exocet missile that exploded into the net.

If that strike was all about sheer venom, the third after the break was a thing of beauty. Wayne Rooney and Ronaldo had continued to pepper Almunia's goal with shots, and they were at the sharp end of a glorious move. Park played his part, too, but Rooney's unselfish pass allowed Ronaldo, busting a gut to motor into the box, to gleefully side-foot in a classic counter-attacking goal following an Arsenal corner.

'That's the sign of a great player,' Rio Ferdinand said of Rooney's contribution. 'He knows when to shoot and when to pass.' Rooney showed his maturity and discipline by spending much of the game on the left flank as Ronaldo wreaked havoc down the middle.

'When we transferred the ball to Ronaldo, it was a big problem for them,' revealed Sir Alex Ferguson. 'Everyone played for each other. They all played their part. But Ronaldo was the difference.'

Arsenal had barely mustered a threat to Edwin van der Sar's goal, but there was a cruel, late twist waiting to put a dampener on the finest of evenings for United. The manager had sensibly withdrawn Evra and Rooney, as another card would have cost them a place in the final through suspension, but he had reckoned without an awful decision by referee Roberto Rosetti.

The Italian official decided Darren Fletcher fouled Cesc Fabregas when making a perfectly legitimate challenge that showed the true professionalism of a player tracking back diligently, with his team coasting towards the biggest game in European football. Rosetti then produced a red card that would rule the influential Scot out of the final, a consequence ultimately much more damaging than Robin van Persie's successful spot-kick that offered scant consolation to his out-classed colleagues.

'It's a massive game to miss and, over two seasons, Darren has been brilliant,' consoled Rooney. 'If anyone deserves to be there, it is him.'

The Scotland international's absence was sorely felt in Rome as Barcelona were able to take control with their passing game, with many pundits suggesting that Fletcher's ability to work tirelessly in closing down the opposition could have proved crucial on the big night.

## THE TEAMS

**Arsenal:** Almunia; Sagna, Toure, Djourou, Gibbs (Eboue 45); Walcott (Bendtner 63), Fabregas, Song, Nasri; van Persie (Vela 79), Adebayor

**Subs not used:** Fabianski, Silvestre, Diaby, Denilson

**Goalscorer:** van Persie 76 (pen)

**Manchester United:** van der Sar; O'Shea, Ferdinand, Vidic, Evra (Rafael 65); Fletcher, Carrick, Anderson (Giggs 63), Park, Rooney (Berbatov 66); Ronaldo

**Subs not used:** Kuszczak, Evans, Scholes, Tevez

**Goalscorers:** Park 8, Ronaldo 11, 61

# 26 MANCHESTER UNITED 4 REAL MADRID 3

Champions League quarter-final, second leg
23 April 2003
Old Trafford, Manchester

## A MOST GLORIOUS FAILURE

'This will be our greatest challenge,' Sir Alex Ferguson warned as United prepared to welcome Real Madrid's Galacticos to Old Trafford. Zidane, Raul, Figo, Ronaldo et al also had the travel insurance of a 3-1 lead in their baggage as they sought to seal their passage to the Champions League semi-finals.

### WHAT THE PAPERS SAID

'Ferguson's men were always chasing the game – but what a chase, what a game! United won on the night, Real on aggregate but football won overall. Here over 90 spellbinding minutes was a feast fit for the watching Alfredo Di Stefano and Sir Bobby Charlton, legends of a glorious bygone age thrilling to the fast-moving feats of the modern generation. Everywhere they looked in this intoxicating unfolding drama, sublime sub-plots and virtuoso displays abounded.'

Henry Winter, *Daily Telegraph*

Reflecting on the Reds' first-leg humbling in the Estadio Santiago Bernabeu, the United manager conceded: 'They mesmerised at times; we could have lost by more. But we've a ray of hope and if we score first in the return it will be very interesting.

'Raul is the best player in the world at the moment – I hope he doesn't travel. Failing that, we'll try and stop him coming into the country.' While the manager's hopeful quip was answered – the Spaniard's appendix operation prevented border control from getting involved – Vicente Del Bosque was hardly short of firepower in Raul's absence.

After dominating the 2002 World Cup with Brazil, Ronaldo again demonstrated his affinity with the grandest stages as he hogged the spotlight at the Theatre of Dreams, despite a rousing display from the hosts amid a game where defending was apparently outlawed.

Early on, Ronaldo latched on to Guti's through-ball and caught Fabien Barthez unawares with a snapshot inside the Frenchman's near post, heralding a spell of sustained dominance from the visitors that carried almost to the interval. Just before the break, however, came a lifeline for United. Ole Gunnar Solskjaer – starting on the right flank ahead of David Beckham – reached the ball ahead of Iker Casillas and squared for Ruud van Nistelrooy to tap home.

Game on? Never quite, sadly. Ronaldo struck his second early in the second half, tapping home after Real put together a move that pulled United's defence this way and that. Though Ivan Helguera quickly levelled matters with a staggeringly impudent flicked own-goal, Ronaldo completed his hat-trick with a rasping 25-yard dipper.

The Brazilian's subsequent substitution sparked two events: a standing ovation from all corners of Old Trafford, and a late fightback from the hosts, led by United substitute Beckham. The England skipper crashed home a marvellous free-kick via the underside of Casillas's crossbar, then chased the ball over the line after Helguera's radar again went haywire.

Time remained for the unlikeliest of comebacks, but the final opportunity came and went when Beckham arrowed another free-kick just over the bar, leaving the Reds eliminated and exhausted, yet quietly compensated after playing their part in such a gleaming advertisement for the game.

## THE TEAMS

**Manchester United:** Barthez; O'Shea, Ferdinand, Brown, Silvestre (P.Neville 79); Solskjaer, Butt, Keane (Fortune 82), Giggs; Veron (Beckham 63); van Nistelrooy

**Subs not used:** Ricardo, Blanc, Forlan, Fletcher

**Goalscorers:** van Nistelrooy 42, Helguera 52 (og), Beckham 71, 84

**Real Madrid:** Casillas; Salgado, Hierro, Helguera, Roberto Carlos; Makelele; Figo (Pavon 88), Zidane, Guti, McManaman (Portillo 69); Ronaldo (Solari 67)

**Subs not used:** Cesar, Morientes, Flavio, Cambiasso

**Goalscorer:** Ronaldo 12, 50, 59

# 25

# MANCHESTER UNITED 2
# FC BARCELONA 1

**European Cup-Winners' Cup final**
**15 May 1991**
**De Kuip Stadium, Rotterdam**

# SINGING IN THE RAIN

'I wanted to show the football fans of Barcelona the real Mark Hughes, not the one booted out of town as a flop,' grinned Mark Hughes. The sight of the white-clad striker was fittingly spectral as his match-winning double delivered a resounding message to his former employers and gave United a winning return to European football.

Hughes's stint at Camp Nou was a short, unhappy chapter of an epic career, and his rapid return to Old Trafford had coaxed his finest form back into the spotlight. The Welshman would establish himself as the man for United's biggest occasions over the course of his second period at the club, and Barcelona felt his full, considerable force in the teeming Rotterdam rain.

United had performed well to win the FA Cup in 1990 and gone all the way in the first year since English clubs were allowed back into Europe after the five-year ban following Heysel, but still Barcelona were clear favourites – even though they were missing goalkeeper Andoni Zubizaretta and key striker Hristo Stoichkov.

After a cagey hour of finely poised play, the game sprang into life. With Barça expecting Clayton Blackmore to hammer a trademark shot from a free-kick, as he had done to great effect during the earlier rounds, Bryan Robson instead clipped the ball into the box where Steve Bruce headed goalwards. Hughes made sure with the final touch before it crossed the line.

Such a strike was never going to be sufficient for Hughes to claim payback on his former employers and, when Robson chipped the ball through to him seven minutes later, his opportunity arrived. Carlos Busquets raced unexpectedly from his goal and succeeded in driving the striker wide. 'A chance for Hughes,' commentated the late Brian Moore. 'Maybe not now.' Wrong. The powerful hitman unleashed a venomous angled drive that thundered into the unguarded goal. 'Once I rounded the goalkeeper, I knew I wasn't going to miss,' he stated.

Any thoughts of a nerve-free finale vanished when Ronald Koeman squeezed a free-kick past a barely fit Les Sealey, who could only push it against an upright and into the net. Nando earned a red card for rugby-tackling Hughes as he hunted a hat-trick but, even with ten men, Barcelona pushed forward as the final whistle approached.

A rare mistake by Bruce allowed substitute Antonio Pinilla to dance his way around Sealey and tee up Michael Laudrup, only for Blackmore to clear off the line. The final whistle duly prompted ecstatic renditions of 'Always Look on the Bright Side of Life' on the terraces and Bruce was able to breathe again. 'If that had gone in, I'd have never been allowed back into Manchester,' he admitted. 'That game was the start of big things for United.'

## THE TEAMS

**Manchester United:** Sealey; Irwin, Bruce, Pallister, Blackmore; Phelan, Robson, Ince, Sharpe; McClair, Hughes

**Subs not used:** Walsh, Donaghy, Webb, Robins, Wallace

**Goalscorer:** Hughes 67, 74

**FC Barcelona:** Busquets; Nando, Alexanco (Pinilla 72), Koeman, Ferrer; Bakero, Goicoechea, Eusebio, Laudrup; Salinas, Beguiristain

**Subs not used:** Angoy, Serna, Soler, Zamora

**Goalscorer:** Koeman 80

# 24

## LIVERPOOL 1
## MANCHESTER UNITED 2

**FA Cup final**
**21 May 1977**
**Wembley Stadium, London**

# BEWARE OF THE UNDERDOGS

Embarrassed by Second Division Southampton in the FA Cup final a year earlier, United made good on manager Tommy Docherty's promise to return to Wembley in 1977 and win the cup, upsetting the mighty Liverpool and derailing the Merseysiders' bid for the Treble.

### WHAT THE PAPERS SAID

'The stealthy goal burglars of Manchester United brought their guile to Wembley's Jubilee final and went away with the most famous piece of silver of them all, the FA Cup. I hope the soccer chroniclers record more than the statistics. Here was a game of such grandeur, so memorable for its sportsmanship and grace, that British football can proudly reflect that the occasion was stage-managed to perfection.'

James Mossop, *Sunday Express*

Confirmed First Division champions on the final day of the season, Liverpool arrived at Wembley brimming with confidence and with their first European Cup final looming on the horizon. The spring in their step was apparent in the opening

exchanges, as was United's determination, characterised by Martin Buchan, playing despite injury and hurling himself into blocks and challenges.

While Liverpool were repeatedly thwarted by such last-ditch heroics, United's counter-attacking menace was always lurking. Ray Clemence produced a full-length save to fend away Gordon Hill's belting effort and Stuart Pearson could only half-hit a shot straight at the England goalkeeper.

Clemence's United counterpart, Alex Stepney, produced the save of the match just before the interval, plunging to turn Ray Kennedy's goalbound header around the post. While the break was reached without score, the goals began flowing soon after the restart.

Kevin Keegan's errant header was redirected by Sammy McIlroy to Jimmy Greenhoff, who neatly nodded on to release Pearson. The striker's first-time shot was uncharacteristically allowed in at the near post by Clemence, yet familiarly celebrated by the striker's trademark fist-pumping salute.

Pearson had failed to find the net in United's run to the final, but had

Hat-trick hero Lee Sharpe celebrates in November 1990 as United put six past the Gunners at Highbury.

Best and Law in tandem, as the Scot scores one of the goals that gave United victory over Liverpool in April 1965 to set them on their way to the league title.

As ever, Roy Keane was in control of the situation in this famous battle against Arsenal in February 2005 – a game that was almost won in the tunnel before kick-off.

Who would ever bet against Cantona missing a penalty? Dennis Wise found out to his cost as United secured their first Double in 1994.

No way through this time for two-goal Niall Quinn, as the Reds roar back from 2-0 down to win the derby in November 1993.

Ole Gunnar Solskjaer forgot all about team instructions to keep the ball, and kept on putting it in the back of the net instead as he scored four as a substitute against Nottingham Forest in February 1999.

Alex Ferguson and Barcelona boss Louis van Gaal pitted their wits against each other in a compelling 3-3 draw at the Camp Nou in November 1998.

Mark Hughes scores the decisive goal in the 1985 FA Cup semi-final replay against Liverpool. It was a fierce contest in which only the tough thrived.

Wayne Rooney slots home to put United into the lead for the first time in their crucial game against Everton in the run-in to the 2007 title.

Newcastle's Shay Given slumps in despair as Paul Scholes wheels away to celebrate another goal in United's 6-2 victory in April 2003.

Early in the second half, George Best completes his hat-trick against Northampton Town in the 1970 FA Cup fifth round. Unfortunately for the hosts, he was only half-done.

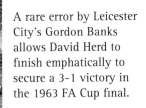

A rare error by Leicester City's Gordon Banks allows David Herd to finish emphatically to secure a 3-1 victory in the 1963 FA Cup final.

Gary Pallister had to be at his very best to help United finally overcome Juventus in this October 1997 Champions League tie.

Denis Law lurks menacingly in the box as United emphatically beat West Ham United 6-1 to secure the 1967 league title.

Captain Johnny Carey leads his side off the Old Trafford pitch after the Reds had beaten Arsenal 6-1 to secure their first league title in over 40 years.

Eric Cantona volleys home against Newcastle United in March 1996 after a great cross from 19-year-old Phil Neville. Perhaps the Reds could win something with kids after all.

One down, two to go: the Reds celebrate winning the 1999 Premier League title after beating Tottenham Hotspur in a tense encounter.

Andy Cole holds on to the match ball after scoring one of his five goals on a day when United set a Premier League record by beating Ipswich Town 9-0 in March 1995.

Twenty-six years of hurt is brought to an end as Steve Bruce and Bryan Robson lift the Premier League trophy in May 1993 – few could have predicted how many more titles would follow.

Dwight Yorke celebrates on a day when his hat-trick helped United to a crushing 6-1 victory over title rivals Arsenal in February 2001.

Gary Neville prevents another attack from Liverpool dangerman Michael Owen in the fourth round of the 1999 FA Cup. United's late show set a theme for the rest of the season.

David May celebrates scoring the first goal against Porto in the Champions League quarter-final, as he cranks up the atmosphere another notch at Old Trafford in 1997.

Dennis Viollet and Tommy Taylor (right) challenge for the ball at Highbury on 1 February 1958 – the 5-4 thriller was the last time the Busby Babes played together in England.

Rio Ferdinand celebrates as United crush Arsenal at the Emirates Stadium in the semi-finals of the 2009 Champions League.

David Beckham aims another free-kick over the Real Madrid wall as he tries to complete the most remarkable of comebacks in April 2003 against the club he would soon join.

United and Barcelona line up in Rotterdam for the European Cup-Winners' Cup final of 1991. While the flames glowed on the terraces, it was Sparky who lit up the night.

Martin Buchan's heroic leadership and fearless work in defence helped underdogs United beat Liverpool in the 1977 FA Cup final.

answered his pre-match critics with a simple promise: 'I'm saving it for Wembley.' Up on the gantry, BBC commentator John Motson was in similarly prophetic mood, warning: 'There's a saying in football that Liverpool are at their most dangerous when they're behind.' Seven seconds later, Liverpool levelled. Joey Jones's long ball forward was controlled by Jimmy Case, who swivelled on the edge of the United area to power a finish high past Stepney.

No matter, as the Reds retook the lead two and a half minutes later. Lou Macari's flick-on landed between Jimmy Greenhoff and Liverpool defender Tommy Smith, who failed to deal with the situation and only teed up Macari. The Scot's close-range effort ended up in the net, but only via a sizable, looping deflection off Greenhoff.

The game's madcap tempo inevitably lulled, but Liverpool recovered to mount a strong finish. Case prompted another full-length save from Stepney, who fielded a flurry of speculative efforts as the Merseysiders grew increasingly desperate until, joyously, the final whistle heralded the Reds' triumph.

A year after being on the receiving end of an upset, Docherty's side had switched roles and taken the spoils.

Liverpool would have to settle for a double, beating Borussia Mönchengladbach in Rome, but nothing could detract from the glory of taking the FA Cup back to Old Trafford.

'After the disappointment of losing to Southampton at Wembley the previous year, the Doc had promised our fans that we would be back to lift the trophy this time around, so the FA Cup meant even more to us than usual,' revealed Buchan. 'As we ran round Wembley with the cup, my mind went back to the year before and Doc's words. To do it against Liverpool was incredible, as sweet as it could be.'

## THE TEAMS

**Liverpool:** Clemence; Neal, Hughes, Smith, Jones; Kennedy, Case, McDermott, Heighway; Johnson (Callaghan 64), Keegan

**Goalscorer:** Case 53

**Manchester United:** Stepney; Nicholl, Buchan, B.Greenhoff, Albiston; Coppell, Macari, McIlroy, Hill (McCreery 81); Pearson, J.Greenhoff

**Goalscorers:** Pearson 51, J.Greenhoff 55

# 23 MANCHESTER UNITED 8 ARSENAL 2

**Premier League**
**28 August 2011**
**Old Trafford, Manchester**

## GUNNED DOWN

### WHAT THE PAPERS SAID

'If no mercy was shown to Arsenal it was not simply because United lusted for this rout of a fellow Champions League club. These are footballers who must be utterly sure they will be sidelined if they offer anything less to the club than every trace of ability they have within them.'

Kevin McCarra, *Guardian*

As United were to discover in the dying throes of the 2011-12 season, football can be a cruel business. Certainly, there was an element of brutality about the way the Reds humiliated a weakened Arsenal team that even brought sympathy from Sir Alex Ferguson towards old foe Arsène Wenger.

'I think it's unfair to criticise him,' stressed the supportive Scot, having just inflicted the most emphatic defeat of the Frenchman's reign as Gunners manager. 'The job he's done for Arsenal and the philosophy he has – he has given Arsenal some very entertaining players.' Most of the entertainment on view on a sunny afternoon in Manchester, however, was provided by the hosts.

The context of the afternoon was clear – City had just inflicted a remarkable 5-1 defeat on Tottenham and the foundations were laid for a two-horse race for the title involving the Manchester teams. If the gauntlet had been thrown by Roberto Mancini's side, this was United's way of picking it up and hurling it back across Manchester.

United's early superiority was rewarded when Danny Welbeck looped a header over Wojciech Szczesny after baffling hesitancy in the visitors' defence, although Robin van Persie had a chance to level matters when Jonny Evans tugged Theo Walcott's shirt. David De Gea dived to the rescue, however, plunging to his right to turn away the Dutchman's attempt.

Moments later, Ashley Young pounced on a loose clearance 25 yards out, steadied himself and had already started his celebratory run by the time the ball arced its way beautifully past Szczesny's despairing fingertips. The Polish keeper at least got a hand to a subsequent Wayne Rooney effort from a free-kick but could not keep it out, although

Walcott's drilled effort in first-half stoppage time added a modicum of uncertainty over the outcome.

That was ended when Rooney repeated his free-kick routine from the first half, this time bending the ball away from Szczesny. Victory assured, United set about hammering home their dominance. Rooney prodded through to Nani, whose impudent chipped finish underlined the gulf in confidence between the two teams.

Substitute Ji-sung Park, so regularly the scourge of the Gunners, exchanged passes with Young to sweep in a left-footed shot for number six and even a close-range volley by van Persie failed to put a dampener on proceedings. Indeed, it only stirred the champions to greater heights.

Carl Jenkinson was spared further examination of his credentials at the back when he received a second yellow card for a blatant foul on Javier Hernandez, before Walcott tripped Patrice Evra inside the box to allow Rooney a hat-trick chance, which he duly took. Young rubbed salt in the wounds by bending another spectacular shot beyond Szczesny in stoppage time, and only the final whistle was able to prevent United from inflicting greater damage on one of the most one-sided encounters Old Trafford has witnessed.

## THE TEAMS

**Manchester United:** De Gea; Jones, Smalling, Evans, Evra; Nani (Park 68), Cleverley, Anderson (Giggs 68), Young; Rooney, Welbeck (Hernandez 35)

**Subs not used:** Lindegaard, Ferdinand, Fabio, Berbatov

**Goalscorers:** Welbeck 22, Young 28, 90, Rooney 41, 64, 82 pen, Nani 67, Park 70

**Arsenal:** Szczesny; Jenkinson, Djourou, Koscielny, Traore; Rosicky, Ramsey, Coquelin (Oxlade-Chamberlain 62), Walcott (Lansbury 83); Arshavin, van Persie (Chamakh 83)

**Subs not used:** Fabianski, Miquel, Ozyakup, Sunu

**Goalscorers:** Walcott 45, van Persie 74

# 22 MANCHESTER UNITED 5
# MANCHESTER CITY 0

**Premier League**
**10 November 1994**
**Old Trafford, Manchester**

## DEMOLITION DERBY

Revenge, the somewhat menacing old adage assures us, is a dish best served cold. Five years seemed ample time, then, for Alex Ferguson to cool and store the mortification of seeing his side torn apart by Manchester City, before exacting an equally chastening thrashing on the men from Maine Road.

Speaking to *The Times*'s Hugh McIlvanney shortly after the Reds's 5-1 derby defeat of 1989, the United manager confided: 'Believe me, what I have felt in the last week you wouldn't think should happen in football. Every time somebody looks at me, I feel I have betrayed that man. After such a result, you feel as if you have to sneak round corners, feel as if you are some kind of criminal ... But I mean to be here making a success of things three years from now.'

Half a decade on and chasing a third successive Premier League title, United were still reeling from their Champions League mauling at Barcelona when Brian Horton's side rocked up at Old Trafford. In confident mood after their side's goal-laden start to the season, the away end was well stocked with Barcelona shirts and scarves. Not a wise move.

After an even opening to the game, United landed the first blow when Andrei Kanchelskis arced a magnificent 40-yard pass into the path of Eric Cantona, whose velvet first touch brought the ball under control, before his second rifled it beyond City keeper Simon Tracey.

The Blues loanee came under increasing pressure as confidence flowed back into United's play, and he was hardly helped when, on the stroke of half time, Kanchelskis opened his account with a close-range shot which struck Terry Phelan and squirmed inside Tracey's near post. While City might have been expected to fly out of the traps in the second period, they merely sat back and seemingly awaited the United onslaught. In those terms, they wouldn't be disappointed.

Kanchelskis and Phelan duelled again in the second period, racing to catch Cantona's flick-on, but while Tracey was equal to the Russian's first shot, the rebound fell perfectly for a simple tap-in. Ditto the Reds' next goal, scored by Mark Hughes with a dismissive toe-poke after his first effort had been blocked by Michel Vonk.

Both sets of supporters knew what was at stake if United scored again. Reds craved it, Blues dreaded it. Teasingly, Hughes missed a sitter before, in stoppage time, along it came. Kanchelskis and Cantona played an enormous one-two on the break, culminating in the winger's shot being saved by Tracey, before the rebound was tucked home to send Old Trafford wild.

While three points provided the evening's immediate focus, the result resonated sufficiently to shake off a past that had haunted the red half of Manchester. 'Derbies are so important because they mean so much to local people,' stressed the manager, having set the record straight after five years of reminders. 'That was a great performance. We looked sharp from the start and some of our football was absolutely brilliant.'

## THE TEAMS

**Manchester United:** Schmeichel; Keane, Bruce, Pallister, Irwin; Kanchelskis, McClair, Ince, Giggs (Scholes 46); Hughes, Cantona

**Subs not used:** Walsh, G.Neville

**Goalscorers:** Cantona 24, Kanchelskis 43, 47, 89, Hughes 70

**Manchester City:** Tracey; Edghill, Vonk, I.Brightwell, Phelan; Summerbee, Lomas, Flitcroft, Beagrie; Quinn, Walsh

**Subs not used:** Burridge, D.Brightwell, Mike

# MANCHESTER UNITED 3
# ASTON VILLA 2

**Premier League**
**5 April 2009**
**Old Trafford, Manchester**

# THE STUFF OF DREAMS

If you'd read the script, you wouldn't have believed it. United, punch-drunk and reeling in a thrilling title battle with perennial rivals Liverpool, were saved in the unlikeliest circumstances as unknown teenager 'Kiko' Macheda delivered a last-gasp knockout blow on his debut.

## WHAT THE PAPERS SAID

'Macheda's winner felt like a seminal moment in the life of a great club: it curled past Brad Friedel like Norman Whiteside's winner flew past Neville Southall in the 1985 FA Cup final. That it was scored by a 17-year-old on his debut made it remarkable; that it came in the 93rd minute of a match United simply had to win was extraordinary. The names change, the generations come and go, but the drama associated with this club remains the same.'

Sam Wallace, *Independent*

Few among the sell-out Old Trafford crowd, and the millions watching around the world, had heard of the 17-year-old Italian, who earlier in the week had bagged a hat-trick for the Reds' Reserves at Newcastle.

After his senior bow, however, he was forever etched in club folklore.

Staggering into the game after back-to-back defeats to Liverpool and Fulham, and hampered by suspensions and injuries, the visit of Aston Villa was a must-win encounter. Furthermore, the Reds' longstanding lead at the head of the table had been overcome by the Merseysiders' injury-time win at Craven Cottage, after which the travelling support vigorously opined: 'We're gonna win the league.'

United's task was stark, and there was little sense of the drama that was to follow when they went ahead early on. Cristiano Ronaldo expertly curled one into the top corner after a free-kick, awarded when Brad Friedel handled James Milner's backpass, was tapped to him by Ryan Giggs.

But Villa battled back and deservedly drew level when Gareth Barry's cross was headed in by John Carew with the defence all at sea and Edwin van der Sar flat-footed. A nightmare scenario gradually unfolded after the break, when Carew ambled forward and drifted in a dangerous cross. Van der Sar was beaten to it by Gabriel Agbonlahor, who nodded into the unguarded net to silence the majority of fans inside Old Trafford.

United had to respond, and a neat build-up ended with Michael Carrick finding Ronaldo, who produced a slide-rule finish from the edge of the box, firing narrowly inside Friedel's left-hand post, but a draw was still insufficient for the Reds with ten minutes remaining. 'In those situations, I gamble,' stated Sir Alex Ferguson. 'Winning is the name of the game at this club. Risks are part of football and this club has been that way for a long time.'

Macheda had already been introduced from the bench, and another fledgling substitute, striker Danny Welbeck, would have been the hero but for a superb save from Friedel, who also denied Darren Fletcher.

In the third of five added minutes, however, the American was given no chance by United's Roman rookie. Receiving Giggs's pass just inside the Villa box, Macheda controlled and set himself in one adroit motion, before sweeping in an unbelievable drive of unerring accuracy. Fear, despair, relief and joy blended in a cocktail of bedlam as Old Trafford shook in disbelief.

A hero was born, and the youngster enjoyed the limelight, kissing Sky Sports's camera at the final whistle and admitting: 'I think this is the day of my dreams.' Even in an arena as befitting as the Theatre of Dreams, Macheda's reverie seemed far-fetched.

## THE TEAMS

**Manchester United:** van der Sar; Neville, O'Shea, Evans, Evra; Nani (Macheda 61), Carrick, Fletcher, Ronaldo, Giggs; Tevez (Welbeck 87)

**Subs not used:** Foster, Park, Gibson, Martin, Eckersley

**Goalscorers:** Ronaldo 14, 80, Macheda 90+3

**Aston Villa:** Friedel; L.Young, Cuellar, Davies, Shorey; Milner (Reo-Coker 76), Petrov, Barry, A.Young; Carew, Agbonlahor

**Subs not used:** Guzan, Delfouneso, Knight, Salifou, Gardner, Albrighton

**Goalscorers:** Carew 30, Agbonlahor 58

# 20 MANCHESTER UNITED 2
# CHELSEA 1

**Premier League**
**8 May 2011**
**Old Trafford, Manchester**

## CHELSEA POWER SHOW

United's bid to bag a fourth straight Premier League title had come unstuck against Chelsea at Old Trafford in April 2010. Just over a year on, Carlo Ancelotti's side pitched up in Manchester looking to repeat the feat and retain the title themselves. Instead, they were on the receiving end of a devastating show of authority from Sir Alex Ferguson's side.

The Reds all but wrapped up title number 19 with a pulsating display that set hearts racing and swelled the pride of any United supporter watching on. Chelsea were a goal behind in a minute, two down after 23 minutes and could consider themselves fortunate to stagger off the field at full time without taking an almighty pummelling.

Defeat for the Reds at Arsenal, between two Champions League semi-final victories over Schalke, had allowed Ancelotti's reigning champions to cut United's longstanding lead to three points with as many games remaining. However, home and away victories over the Blues in the previous round had filled Sir Alex with confidence, and his decision to rest a host of players for the second leg against the Germans

was validated by comfortable progress.

'The European Cup is the trophy Chelsea wanted most and we knocked them out of that,' he said pre-match, pointedly. 'We've played them three times, beaten them twice and I think we've been the better team. We have to prove that again on Sunday. We're used to the title races going to the wire. The fans' fingernails are withered away anyway, but we should be all right with our experience.'

Chelsea's previous Premier League visit to Old Trafford had yielded that pivotal 2-1 victory which ended the Reds' run of successive titles, and had been conducted amid a nervy atmosphere in the stands. This time around, M16 was aglow with expectation pre-match and aflame with stridence just 37 seconds in.

With the game's very first attack, Ji-sung Park threaded through a pass for Javier Hernandez, which David Luiz failed to intercept, giving the little Mexican time and space to slot a typically clinical finish inside Petr Cech's post before sprinting away in delirious celebration. Suitably galvanised by their early advantage, there was no let-up from United.

The non-stop Park achieved apparent omnipresence, Chicharito spooked Luiz and John Terry with every darting run, Ryan Giggs and Michael Carrick dominated midfield and Wayne Rooney pulled all the attacking strings with one of his finest displays for the club. Cech had to hurl himself full-length to turn away an audacious 35-yard fizzer from the England striker, then a similarly powerful effort from the edge of the area from Park. He was a lone bastion of resistance in a meek display from the visitors, who were presently two goals behind when Giggs jinked past Salomon Kalou and crossed for Nemanja Vidic to head home.

The shell-shocked visitors were briefly shaken into life and tested Edwin van der Sar through Kalou's header and a Didier Drogba free-kick, but the interval came and went with United still well on top. Soothed by their manager and cushioned by their two-goal lead, the hosts played with greater refinement after the restart, looking to hit the Blues on the break wherever possible. Such raids may have yielded penalties as Frank Lampard survived a handball shout and Terry chopped down Antonio Valencia, both without censure. However, a potential plot-twist loomed when Lampard volleyed home Branislav Ivanovic's knock-down with 22 minutes remaining.

Irritated by the needless concession, United immediately sought to safeguard victory. A quickfire quartet of Rooney efforts were all thwarted – two brilliantly blocked by Alex, one dragged wide and one parried away by Cech – before Chicharito could only head

Valencia's thunderous cross over the bar from four yards.

Those spurned chances sprinkled mercy on the scoreline, but the increasingly nervy home supporters cared not a jot when the final whistle sounded, and cranked up the volume one last time with a primal roar to accompany the final whistle. 'It was the best atmosphere at Old Trafford that I've known for a long time,' said Rio Ferdinand. 'The fans were up for it. They knew what that result meant and they knew it could be a pivotal moment in the season. The roar before the game kicked off, the chanting in the warm-up ... there was just a really good buzz about the place and the early goal managed to pump things up even more.

'Everything clicked and it was good to be a part of it. I think the result flattered Chelsea a little bit. It could have been four or five. We had countless opportunities to score goals – enough chances to win two or three games – and it was great to show everybody who the best team in the league was.'

Six days later, Ferdinand and his colleagues had the Premier League trophy to lend further weight to an already compelling case.

## THE TEAMS

**Manchester United:** van der Sar; Fabio (Smalling 88), Ferdinand, Vidic, O'Shea (Evans 46); Valencia, Carrick, Giggs, Park; Rooney, Hernandez

**Subs not used:** Kuszczak, Anderson, Berbatov, Nani, Scholes

**Goalscorers:** Hernandez 1, Vidic 23

**Chelsea:** Cech; Ivanovic, Luiz (Alex 46), Terry, Cole; Essien, Mikel (Ramires 46), Lampard; Kalou (Torres 62), Drogba, Malouda

**Subs not used:** Turnbull, Ferreira, Anelka, Benayoun

**Goalscorer:** Lampard 68

# 19

## MANCHESTER UNITED 1
## LIVERPOOL 0

FA Cup final
11 May 1996
Wembley Stadium, London

## THE DOUBLE DOUBLE

Having hauled United to the Premier League title with a spate of invaluable late-season goals, Eric Cantona gilded his place in Reds folklore by enlivening a damp squib of an FA Cup final with a stunning late winner.

Until the Frenchman's decisive intervention, the Wembley showpiece was largely notable for the cream Armani suits that bedecked Liverpool's squad pre-match. But, if anybody was going to break the deadlock, in a cagey encounter stifled by Liverpool manager Roy Evans's decision to play with five at the back, it was going to be Cantona.

Occasionally erratic goalkeeper David James opted to meet a teasing David Beckham corner with an unconvincing punch that reached only the edge of the Liverpool area. While mere mortals would have controlled the loose ball and, almost certainly, been closed down by a sea of white and green shirts, Cantona's thought process was on another level.

As the ball struck Ian Rush and approached the Frenchman at an awkward height, he simply took a step back to allow the execution of a volley at knee height. It travelled through the forest of defenders like an arrow and was the perfect end to a season which, for the Frenchman – suspended for clashing with Crystal Palace fan Matthew Simmons 16 months earlier – had started with a goal against the Merseysiders in October 1995.

'The one time he had a little bit of space and the one time their keeper made a mistake, he punished them,' enthused Sir Bobby Charlton. 'It was great technique, which he has always had. Eric is brilliant.'

The match itself was one of few chances, as both sides looked apprehensive with so much at stake. United's fans were unperturbed, entertaining themselves with boisterous renditions of 'We won the football league again, down by the Riverside', in reference to the title being clinched at Middlesbrough six days earlier.

Andy Cole may have misfired in attack at Wembley, screwing one early opportunity wide, but his performance did not warrant one newspaper questioning afterwards if it would be his last game for the club. Indeed, the man who played a key role in the Treble three years later went on to make a further 214 appearances for the Reds, hitting the net another 98 times.

The temperature rose when David Beckham's crisp drive, set up by Ryan Giggs, forced James into acrobatic action, and the oft-criticised keeper also blocked a Cantona volley after the Frenchman had battled with Jason McAteer to meet a Beckham cross. At the other end, the Merseysiders barely tested Peter Schmeichel, with Jamie Redknapp blazing a rare attempt over the bar.

## WHAT THE PAPERS SAID

'If ever proof was needed that the devil inside has been exorcised for the good of Eric Cantona, it was the trail of Scouse spittle trickling down his red shirt as he climbed the 39 steps to his own personal heaven. Little more than a year ago, less provocation launched him over the barricades and into sporting infamy. Now, a restrained Gallic glare withered his tormentors before he completed the climb to hoist the FA Cup.'

Colin Stewart, *The Scotsman*

Roy Keane snapped into tackles and bristled with aggression throughout to earn the Man of the Match award, squaring up to Robbie Fowler at one point and refusing to countenance the idea of defeat. Keane commented afterwards: 'People get involved in one or two niggly incidents, but that was the end of it; it was over and done with. You'll never take out the determination in my game because that's my strength. I can't rely too much on skill, because I haven't got much, so I've got to look

to my determination and my will to win. If you take that away, then I'm only half the player.'

It looked as though extra time was inevitable until Phil Babb's needless concession of a corner led to Cantona's dramatic intervention, and there was to be no response from Liverpool. The game's stunning denouement negated an otherwise forgettable afternoon, which might have been sullied post-match as a Liverpool fan spat at Cantona, while another aimed a punch towards Alex Ferguson as the pair climbed the famous Wembley steps.

'Don't bother about that,' stressed the manager. 'There was nothing silly. If someone had a swing at me, he obviously doesn't know how good I am at fighting. The way I feel right now, I could climb Mount Everest with my slippers on!'

Nobody deserved the glory more than Cantona, who led from the front all season, and yet it showed the measure of the man that he offered regular skipper Bruce the chance to lift the cup. 'He said no,' explained the ex-Leeds striker. 'So I went up and I am very proud. I always thought I could succeed with my pals but that was special, historic.'

The youth products that looked up to the most charismatic of figures were in no doubt that this was always going to be Cantona's day. 'It had to be him,' grinned Beckham. 'It was written in the stars that way. When you consider what he's been through this season – the criticism, the doubts and the pressure he's been under – the way he's come through it has been sensational. I thought that he might just be able to do it, because I know him, I know the sort of person he is. But I don't think anybody else could have shown that character. Nobody else in the world could have done it in the same way. He's unbelievable.'

While more glory would follow for Beckham and his fellow twinkling talents, this match belonged to the maverick majesty of Cantona.

## THE TEAMS

**Manchester United:** Schmeichel; Irwin, May, Pallister, P.Neville; Beckham (G.Neville 90), Keane, Butt, Giggs; Cantona, Cole (Scholes 64)

**Sub not used:** Sharpe

**Goalscorer:** Cantona 85

**Liverpool:** James; McAteer, Scales, Wright, Babb, Jones (Thomas 86); Redknapp, Barnes, McManaman; Collymore (Rush 74), Fowler

**Sub not used:** Warner

# 18 MANCHESTER UNITED 3 ATHLETIC BILBAO 0

**European Cup quarter-final, second leg**
**6 February 1957**
**Maine Road, Manchester**

## THE COMEBACK KIDS

Exactly a year before the Munich disaster cruelly curtailed the Busby Babes, United's vibrant young side delivered a potent pointer of the spirit that would carry the club through its darkest hour.

Beaten in Bilbao by a gifted Athletic side three weeks earlier and faced with a two-goal deficit to overturn, United roared back with a display of pluck and moxie that will be forever enshrined in club folklore. Maine Road, the Reds' temporary home on European Cup nights while Old Trafford's floodlights were constructed, staged an exposition of spirit so overpowering, Bilbao skipper 'Piru' Gainza could only shrug: 'These blokes are magnificent.'

Bilbao, for their part, were no mugs either. Their first-leg display in San Mames had ridiculed a playing surface saturated by pre-match blizzards, and only a cracking late individual effort from Billy Whelan hauled United back to a 3-5 scoreline halfway through the tie. Nine of the Spaniards' 13-man travelling party were full internationals and the team bristled with attacking menace, yet they would rarely be allowed to show it in Manchester.

Usually a fruitful supply line for their forwards, Bilbao's half-back line of Mauri, Jesus Garay and Jose Maria Maguregui was instead employed almost entirely by trying to keep United at bay. With each passing minute that they managed to do so, those of a nervous disposition suffered further. 'I was sitting with Matt [Busby] surrounded by a pile of half-smoked cigarettes,' recalled assistant manager Jimmy Murphy.

Not that the tense spectacle was doing anything to dampen an incredible atmosphere. 'Never, before or since, have I heard Manchester United fans cheer as loudly as they did that night,' recalled Wilf McGuinness, one of the young Reds watching from the sidelines. 'The passion of the crowd was more than our players are used to at home,' remarked Bilbao president Enrique Guzman, who saw his side undone on the stroke of half time.

Duncan Edwards's shot deflected kindly into the path of Dennis Viollet, who took the ball in his stride, edged past the desperate lunge of Bilbao's Garay and buried his shot high into the roof of the net. In the days before away goals, United were a goal from parity.

Bilbao, suddenly in possession of

their shooting boots again, posed greater danger after the break, with Manuel Etura twice going close to beating Ray Wood, but United were riding the crest of a wave and had 'goals' from Whelan and Viollet contentiously disallowed for offside, before hulking striker Tommy Taylor came into his own.

'Tommy was extraordinarily shy,' said Murphy. 'We had a hell of a job persuading him that he was good enough to play in the First Division, but he played some of his best games in the European Cup and this was one of them. The second leg against Bilbao was Tommy's match.'

Moments after thundering a shot against a post, Taylor hauled United back on terms by collecting Eddie Colman's free-kick and sliding a low effort across goalkeeper Carmelo and into the far corner. Bedlam ensued, and had barely subsided when, with six minutes remaining, Taylor again grabbed the game by the scruff of the neck.

Slipping through the gears to glide past Garay – renowned as one of Europe's finest defenders – the United and England striker faked to shoot before nonchalantly slipping the ball to an onrushing Johnny Berry. 'I couldn't even see the goal for players,' recalled the winger, 'but up it went, skimmed the forehead of their right-back and it was in the net. If that right-back had been two inches taller he would have stopped it!'

As the ball nestled high in the Bilbao net, the scenes of celebration were near-feral. 'A goal which tore the linings from 65,000 throats and I dare say nearly burst 65,000 hearts,' remarked one especially graphic match report.

In a fashion that would become a hallmark of achieving deeds the United way – otherwise known as the hard way – the Reds almost contrived to throw away victory, as Gainza pounced on a loose ball in the six-yard box, only to be thwarted as Wood hurled himself at the striker's feet to save the day. Had Gainza scored, the clubs would have reconvened in Paris for a one-legged play-off. 'The last five minutes seemed like hours,' remarked Roger Byrne.

Instead, United held on to register a victory that has stood the test of time as a performance emblematic of Busby's fearless Babes. 'I have never known anything like this in my life,' beamed the manager. 'The thrill of a lifetime. The whole atmosphere of the game was electric. The team – and the crowd – were magnificent. This beat even the ten-nil defeat of Anderlecht. What can I say about the boys, except I'm so very proud of them.'

'I cried when we scored that third goal,' laughed Murphy. 'I don't mind admitting it. Silly, isn't it? But this is the greatest night of my life in soccer.'

'My heart is still galloping,' added goalkeeper Wood, long after the final whistle, while the *Daily Express* took the unprecedented step of awarding the game six out of five stars in its match rating.

While Munich took the Busby Babes from football, nothing will erase the tales of skill, daring and bravery those young Reds exuded every time they took to the field; attributes which never shone brighter than on an unforgettable evening at Maine Road.

## THE TEAMS

**Manchester United:** Wood; Foulkes, Byrne; Colman, Jones, Edwards; Berry, Whelan, Taylor, Viollet, Pegg

**Goalscorers**: Viollet 41, Taylor 70, Berry 84

**Athletic Bilbao:** Carmelo; Orue, Canito; Mauri, Garay, Maguregui; Arteche, Marcaida, Etura, Merodio, Gainza

# 17 MANCHESTER UNITED 4
# MANCHESTER CITY 3

Premier League
20 September 2009
Old Trafford, Manchester

# THE GREATEST DERBY
# OF ALL TIME

Getting what you want is so much sweeter when you're made to doubt that you'll ever have it.

Hence, having apparently thrice thrown away victory over Manchester City amid the inflating importance of the Manchester derby, United's last-gasp triumph led to an explosion of joy rarely matched in Old Trafford's epic history.

For all the money lavished on Mark Hughes's City side – most notably in the returning Carlos Tevez, the headline act in Eastlands' festival of newcomers – it was a player who cost nothing, United's Michael Owen, who made the telling contribution on an afternoon that was instantly catapulted into derby folklore.

The visitors were emerging as a real threat to United's dominance in the city of Manchester and beyond, and arrived at Old Trafford intent on announcing their arrival as the new local force. 'Sometimes you get a noisy neighbour and you have to live with it,' Sir Alex Ferguson reckoned, but the early signs suggested it would be a one-sided affair. After little more than a minute, Patrice Evra's run to

collect a Ryan Giggs throw-in unhinged the City defence and Wayne Rooney danced his way through a crowded box, beating three defenders, to tuck the opener past Shay Given.

Only a mistake by Ben Foster surrendered the advantage, as the keeper was tackled by Tevez when trying to usher the ball back into his penalty area. Tevez, booed after moving across Manchester in controversial fashion, profited from the scruffy piece of play to tee up Gareth Barry, who stroked into an inviting target to punish Foster's error.

Tevez did his best to antagonise his former employers further, but should have scored just before half time when hitting the outside of a post under pressure from Evra, a close pal of the Argentinian's during their time at Old Trafford. Having started the first period so brightly, United repeated the trick after the break, as Darren Fletcher arrived at the far post to head home a centre by Giggs.

All too quickly – and easily, Sir Alex would later lament – Craig Bellamy took advantage of time and space to crack an unstoppable long-range effort into Foster's top corner to quickly level the scores again.

The Reds piled forward in response, but found Given in top form, with Dimitar Berbatov twice denied, once when he seemed certain to find the net with a header. Giggs also brought the best out of the Republic of Ireland number one as the hosts dominated. 'We came out all guns blazing in the second half and played the way that we know we can and the way we should always play,' stressed Sir Alex.

## WHAT THE PAPERS SAID

'The winner was one from the old school, you might say, for the way it shattered and infuriated the new pretenders from across the city. Certainly, one from the old handbook for Owen, who recreated all his predatory glory in one roaring moment that will remain stamped at the core of this freshly intense and bitter rivalry for ages to come.'

John Dillon, *Daily Express*

The approach looked to have spawned victory with ten minutes remaining, as Fletcher again rose highest to repeat his earlier effort, nodding in a Giggs free-kick. Instead, more laxness let City in the back door. Rio Ferdinand was guilty of a rare slip, casually gifting possession to substitute Martin Petrov. The Bulgarian released Bellamy, who showed Ferdinand a clean pair of heels, continued his run past an out-of-position Foster and touched into an empty net.

The Blues frolicked in lengthy celebrations in front of the away end, while Michael Carrick was introduced at the expense of Anderson. Those stoppages contrived to take the game beyond the originally allotted four minutes of added time, and referee Martin Atkinson was still playing when Joleon Lescott's headed clearance reached Giggs, who took stock and quickly spotted that Owen had peeled away into space.

Though the through-ball was immaculate, it took a similarly flawless touch from Owen to bring it under control, before he poked home a finish just before Shaun Wright-Phillips could intervene. Bedlam followed. 'It's one of those few moments in your career that you look back on and think that's great, that was one of the highlights,' admitted United's new signing, having scored only his second goal for the club. 'It was such an entertaining game – one of the best televised games of all time. So to score the winner like that was tremendous.'

Hughes fumed on the touchline as his former club enjoyed the unforgettable climax to a remarkable game. Predictably, he took issue with the amount of stoppage time and made his point to fourth official Alan Wiley. In reality, Owen's shot hit the net 85 seconds over the minimum amount scheduled to be played, and the extra period was later proved to be justified. 'It's not an exact science, but you normally find managers who complain about playing too much or too little stoppage time have lost,' said former World Cup referee Jack Taylor pointedly.

Once the whys and wherefores had

died down, however, the dust settled on a staggering spectacle that took all supporters – and a fair few neutrals – through the wringer. 'We could have won by six or seven,' lamented Sir Alex, 'and the fact we made mistakes probably made it the best derby game of all time. Would we have rather won six-nil or had the greatest-ever derby? I'd rather have won six-nil!'

Perhaps, but then that wouldn't quite have been the United way of doing things. The price of frayed nerves and premature ageing has rarely seemed so inconsequential.

## THE TEAMS

**Manchester United:** Foster; O'Shea, Ferdinand, Vidic, Evra; Park (Valencia 62), Anderson (Carrick 90), Fletcher, Giggs; Berbatov (Owen 78), Rooney

**Subs not used:** Kuszczak, Neville, Evans, Nani

**Goalscorers:** Rooney 2, Fletcher 49, 80, Owen 90+5

**Manchester City:** Given; Richards, Lescott, Toure, Bridge; Wright-Phillips, Barry, De Jong (Petrov 83), Ireland, Bellamy; Tevez

**Subs not used:** Taylor, Zabaleta, Garrido, Sylvinho, Weiss, Ball

**Goalscorers:** Barry 16, Bellamy 52, 90

# 16 MANCHESTER UNITED 7
## AS ROMA 1

**Champions League quarter-final, second leg**
**10 April 2007**
**Old Trafford, Manchester**

# THE MAGNIFICENT SEVEN

Every once in a while, everything clicks. Players, management and fans scale the height of their powers, join forces and tear an unsuspecting opponent apart with a triangular assault of energy, tactics and noise. Poor Roma suffered such a fate on a night when Old Trafford was geared up for an arduous challenge, but instead witnessed an unfeasible exertion of power.

Luciano Spalletti's side were armed with a 2-1 first-leg lead and a revolving formation that had set tactical purists purring, while the legacy of running battles between rival supporters in Rome and travelling Reds' treatment at the hands of Italian police added further subplots to proceedings. When skirmishes were resumed on the Old Trafford forecourt, with riot police intervening, the pre-match atmosphere crackled in anticipation of what lay ahead.

'We wanted to win to dedicate the victory to the fans,' revealed Gabriel Heinze, 'because of all that had gone on in Rome, with all those unfair incidents taking place.' Though

motivated, United entered the game reeling from successive defeats – the first leg in Rome and a shock Premier League reverse at struggling Portsmouth – and depleted in number. Gary Neville, Nemanja Vidic and Louis Saha had suffered long-term injuries, Henrik Larsson's loan had lapsed and Paul Scholes was banned after his red card at the Stadio Olimpico.

That prompted the deployment of the energetic Darren Fletcher in midfield, while Wes Brown deputised at centre-back. So short was Sir Alex Ferguson of senior cover, that he had to stock his bench with youngsters Dong Fangzhuo, Craig Cathcart and Chris Eagles. Roma, meanwhile, were in fine fettle and had an ambitious gameplan of quickly targeting Edwin van der Sar. The Dutchman had been punished by goals after parrying long-range shots both in Italy and at Fratton Park, and visiting skipper Francesco Totti twice came close from 30 yards in the opening five minutes.

Spalletti's fluid formation operated for long periods without a striker, with Totti and Mirko Vucinic dropping deep, facilitating a tactic of finding room and striking from distance. It was from such a position, however, that Michael Carrick cranked the match into overdrive.

Cristiano Ronaldo motored down the right flank before spotting Carrick, with space to advance into. The England midfielder's light first touch worked in his favour, forcing him to dig out a shot without any backlift and catching goalkeeper Doni on his heels. As the ball arced into the net, almost in indulgent slow motion, United were suddenly in charge of the tie. Having wrested it from the visitors, they would never give it back.

The Reds' approach was one of expending masses of energy in order to hustle Roma off their considered stride. It worked. Fletcher and striker Alan Smith – making his first Champions League start in 18 months – resembled hummingbirds as they flitted from opponent to opponent, while young pups Ronaldo and Wayne Rooney struck fear into the visitors with their every touch.

While working breathlessly to gain possession, United were also stunningly efficient once they had won the ball. The evening's second and third goals were remorseless, inescapable acts of team brilliance. Scored two minutes apart, both began in the Reds' area and finished in Doni's net without a Roma player mustering more than a brush of the ball.

Firstly, van der Sar found Brown, whose pass to Rooney was looped up towards Carrick and dismissively sent wide to Heinze. The Argentine instantly found Ryan Giggs, whose curled pass evaded the shoddy efforts of Cristian Chivu, allowing Smith to stroke home a finish. Seven players, seven touches, one unforgettable goal. 'Almost a perfect Champions League goal,' marvelled Sir Alex.

The next was almost as good. A Roma foray was broken up by Fletcher and John O'Shea, with the latter picking out Ronaldo. The Portuguese surged past two challenges before poking the ball to Smith, who found Giggs on the right flank. Given inexplicable space to exploit but with only Rooney and four defenders in the area, the veteran advanced before picking out his cohort to slot home, via Doni's post.

On the stroke of half time, Giggs struck again, feeding Ronaldo to drill home his first goal in the Champions League proper. The precocious youngster needed to wait for only four minutes after the break before his second arrived, a simple tap-in from another immaculate Giggs cross.

The goals continued to pour in, and each bore its own special quality. On the hour, Carrick cracked an unfathomable effort into Doni's top corner and wheeled away with a blend of shock and laughter. Even Roma's plaintive riposte drew applause, as Daniele De Rossi brilliantly hooked in a volley despite facing away from goal, before substitute Patrice Evra rounded off the scoring with a low effort from outside the box.

As a staggering evening's entertainment drew to a close, Sir Alex marvelled: 'It's the greatest night I've had here. The quality was so high that once we scored the second and third, I was thinking: "This could be something big." Our performance in the first half was out of this world; Roma were in shock.'

'We knew we had to start well,' admitted two-goal hero Carrick. 'When we played them over there, they put us under pressure from the word go and we had a hard first twenty minutes, and we wanted to do the same to them. We knew we had the ammunition to score goals, but I

don't think we thought we could score that many and play so well! But it was great to be a part of. Everything clicked. Everything we wanted to go right went right.'

## THE TEAMS

**Manchester United:** van der Sar; O'Shea (Evra 52), Ferdinand, Brown, Heinze; Ronaldo, Fletcher, Carrick (Richardson 73), Giggs (Solskjaer 60); Smith, Rooney

**Subs not used:** Kuszczak, Eagles, Cathcart, Dong

**Goalscorers:** Carrick 12, 60, Smith 17, Rooney 19, Ronaldo 44, 49, Evra 81

**Roma:** Doni; Panucci, Mexes, Chivu, Cassetti; Wilhelmsson (Rosi 88), De Rossi (Faty 86), Vucinic, Pizarro, Mancini (Okaka Chuka 90); Totti

**Subs not used:** Curci, Defendi, Ferrari

**Goalscorer:** De Rossi 69

# 15 REAL MADRID 3 MANCHESTER UNITED 3

European Cup semi-final, second leg
15 May 1968
Estadio Santiago Bernabeu, Madrid

## SILENCING THE BERNABEU

In 1968, facing the mighty Real Madrid, a club that had ruled the continent for half of the European Cup's dozen years was a daunting prospect in any circumstance. Doing so before 125,000 baying, partisan Madridistas in the second leg of a European Cup semi-final and shipping three first-half goals to the Spanish aristocrats would have broken most teams. Indeed, United trudged off the Estadio Santiago Bernabeu pitch at half time a beaten side.

'We walked off the field bewildered,' recalled Paddy Crerand. 'There was no escape. The stadium was so big that everywhere we looked, we saw happy, smiling faces who were revelling in our suffering.' Yet 45 minutes later, the vast majority of the stadium would be gripped by a stunned silence as United, leaning heavily on a 1-0 first-leg lead secured by George Best, ousted Spain's finest with a second-half display of gritted teeth and renewed refusal to surrender meekly.

Mindful of his side's slender advantage, Matt Busby had opted to approach the game with a defensive set-up, with David Sadler and Bill Foulkes helping to repel Real's raids. The latter, a veteran who had been struggling for fitness, had played in the 1957 defeat to Madrid at the same stage of the competition and would later play an unlikely role in the Reds' triumph.

Without knee-injury victim Denis Law, this was always going to be the most serious test of United's European aspirations, and it quickly panned out that way. Amancio headed against the bar and Alex Stepney made a fine stop to keep out Manuel Sanchis's long-range effort. The onslaught continued, and Amancio's controversial free-kick, as referee Antonio Sbardella initially awarded a goal-kick, was nodded downwards past Stepney by Pirri for the opening goal.

Although Best occasionally provided evidence of his magnetic control, United were making little impression going forward, with only 18-year-old Brian Kidd really able to assist the Northern Irishman. And the task looked an impossible one when

Francisco Gento pounced after Shay Brennan failed to cut out a long ball down the left flank. The speedy winger bore down on goal and crashed one into the net via Stepney's legs.

## WHAT THE PAPERS SAID

'No transformation I have ever seen could rival this breathtaking drama. For 45 minutes before United marched off the field in triumph, they had appeared to be on the brink of certain defeat.'

Ronald Crowther, *Daily Mail*

The home fans were buoyant, but an unexpected lifeline arrived as John Aston headed a ball back to Tony Dunne in midfield and the defender's speculative punt into the area was inexplicably sliced into his own net by Ignacio Zoco. It silenced the crowd briefly, but they were soon cranking up the volume once more as Nobby Stiles, by now public enemy number one after waging a running battle with Amancio, was booked.

And the fans were soon celebrating the restoration of a crucial two-goal advantage on the night. Best found himself in an unfamiliar right-back role and allowed Sanchis to centre far too easily, with Amancio ramming home after the cross was only partially cleared by Dunne.

'Deep down, I was desperately disappointed and worried at half time, but I had to conceal it,' revealed Busby. 'I told the lads if they took the game to Madrid, went at them, they could beat them.' It had the desired effect, even if it shocked the weary players, who had lost the title race to

Manchester City the previous weekend. 'I could hardly believe my ears,' said Crerand. 'Here was a man asking us to attack when we had been struggling to get a kick.'

Stiles, later left requiring stitches after a Real fan threw a bottle at him when boarding the coach, admitted: 'No one remembered that there was only one goal in the game and Matt didn't moan. He just said go out and enjoy it, and we did.'

Sadler pushed forward and the belief flooded back into the red-shirted heroes. Crerand and Bobby Charlton whistled long-range attempts narrowly off target, but time was starting to run out, with United still trailing 3-2 on aggregate. The breakthrough came when Charlton's free-kick was headed on by Best and Sadler jumped to tuck it into the net on the volley from close range.

The momentum was with United and Madrid started, for once, to waver. Crerand's throw allowed European Footballer of the Year Best to show off his dribbling skills, outfoxing Sanchis and intelligently cutting the ball back for 36-year-old Foulkes, of all people, to find the net with a firm finish.

'As soon as Georgie set off, I knew somehow he would skin that full-back,' recalled Foulkes. 'Something told me, so I ran on a parallel course and, sure enough, there was the ball and there was I. I knew if I took a real swing at it, it would probably finish in the crowd, so I told myself to keep my head and just sidefooted it.'

Stiles still struggles to fathom how the veteran managed to make the run that would bring United closer to landing the holy grail after the agony and torment of losing so many players to the Munich disaster while embarking on a quest to conquer Europe. 'Bill Foulkes told me not to go forward and I wasn't going to argue with him,' said Stiles. 'He got the equaliser – the man who never left defence, and after telling me not to go forward too! I went to celebrate with him, but he was having none of it and told me to get back in defence straight away.'

It was the mindset required to maintain the aggregate lead. All hands were required on deck to keep Real at bay, but the damage had been done with the two goals inside five minutes. The tie had been turned on its head and even the Spanish supermen were unable to conjure up a fourth goal, with Best even forcing a save out of Antonio Betancort on the break.

Charlton, another survivor of Munich, cried when the final whistle halted Real's attempts to retrieve the tie. 'I can't explain how I feel except that it is a wonderful night for United,' he said in the aftermath, while trying to keep his emotions in check.

Having failed at the last-four stage on three occasions, the major hurdle was cleared at the most intimidating of arenas against one of the world's finest teams. 'The greatest night in our history,' exclaimed Busby post-match, but he knew the planning for an even greater one at Wembley could now begin in earnest.

## THE TEAMS

**Real Madrid:** Betancort; Gonzalez, Zunzunegui; Sanchis, Pirri, Zoco; M.Perez, Amancio, Grosso, Velazquez, Gento

**Goalscorers:** Pirri 32, Gento 41, Amancio 45

**Manchester United:** Stepney; Dunne, Brennan; Crerand, Foulkes, Stiles; Best, Kidd, Charlton, Sadler, Aston

**Goalscorers:** Zoco 44 (og), Sadler 73, Foulkes 78

# 14 MANCHESTER UNITED 1 EVERTON 0

**Premier League**
**22 January 1994**
**Old Trafford, Manchester**

## FOOTBALL TAUGHT BY MATT BUSBY

Entertainment. Expression. Enjoyment. The football principles that Sir Matt Busby championed were showcased in a heart-swelling remembrance of the great man against Everton at Old Trafford.

Two days after his death, United's staff, players and fans fought back every gnawing urge to mourn their former manager, and instead celebrated his legacy – football's goodness in microcosm – amid an emotional victory over the Merseysiders. They should have scored six, they might have scored ten, but, ultimately, a solitary Ryan Giggs goal secured a winning tribute to one of the grandest figures in United's history.

Within hours of the news that Sir Matt had lost his battle with cancer, Old Trafford swarmed with supporters of clubs from all over the country. The East Stand forecourt became a carpeted shrine to the Scot's memory, with shirts, scarves, pictures and poems scrawled with tender messages of thanks and tribute.

Club legend Denis Law, signed by Busby and a doting protégé, visited the spreading shrine. 'There were hundreds of people there,' he said, 'and nobody spoke to me. None of the usual joking and cracking. Just a few nods, and silence. Very eerie. Very impressive.'

At the same time, Alex Ferguson admitted that the news had rocked the club's preparations for the game with Everton, even though the decision was taken that the game would go ahead as scheduled: 'People will say: "Life goes on," but it doesn't need to always go on,' he said. 'Tomorrow, I think it should stop for a day because he was a wonderful man, but the game will go on, unfortunately. I'd rather it didn't, to be honest with you.'

As kick-off loomed on match day, the forecourt crowds leaning on crash barriers were 50 deep, each queuing for a private audience with their own debt of gratitude to Sir Matt.

There was some comfort that the great man had finally seen his beloved club crowned champions once again, and United were well on course to repeating the feat in 1993-94, having established a yawning lead over the rest of the Premier League. Victory over the Toffeemen – in only their second league game under the management of Mike Walker – would give the Reds a 16-point lead at the head of the table. However, Alex Ferguson, having digested the situation, insisted: 'I will just tell the players to go out and enjoy it and play the way Sir Matt would have wanted them to play. For once this season, the result is immaterial.'

The Busby family had their say on how the occasion should be conducted, relaying a pre-match message to the 44,750 supporters through stadium announcer Keith Fane. 'Matt always had a smile on his face, even during the last few days in hospital,' they said. 'For champions past and present, please sing the roof off the stadium today.'

The applause rose, fell and ceased shortly afterwards as a lone piper, Terry Carr from the Mount Carmel Pipe Band, led the teams onto the field while playing 'A Scottish Soldier'. A minute's silence was immaculately observed, even by the most grief-stricken supporters, in an astonishing 60 seconds. The only interruption came from the light January wind, which toyed with the black ribbons dangling daintily from the emptiest seat in the house: seat B122, Sir Matt's seat. 'I've experienced some minute's silences before,' Mark Hughes confided afterwards, 'but nothing as intense as that.'

Up on the gantry, BBC commentator Gerald Sinstadt said of the supporters: 'They don't want to be solemn. They know how much they owe Sir Matt Busby and how much they will miss him, but this is a club, above all, that knows that life goes on.' Indeed, it had to. After the second peep of the referee's whistle, Everton's supporters were afforded thunderous applause for their spotless role in proceedings. When the game began, however, United's players were clearly affected by the circumstances, and Peter Schmeichel was forced into fine saves from Neil Moore and Brett Angell.

## WHAT THE PAPERS SAID

'United are truly a magnificent side, a team in the richest tradition of Busby's club; elegant, inventive, adventurous and beset by the decent conviction that the game is first and last about glory. They are forever threatening to do something extravagantly dramatic and enthralling, while, in Alex Ferguson, United are led by a manager who speaks Busby's language. To Everton's absolute credit, they battled the odds with marvellous persistence; shrugging off every escape, every miss, every chance which seemed about to unleash the avalanche. But, on this day above all other, United's victory was not to be denied. For they owed it to that gentle, decent man who established their standards. To the man whose memory the grand old game will forever celebrate and cherish.'

Patrick Collins, *Mail on Sunday*

Yet soon the football was flowing, and fittingly the opening goal came from Giggs, the youngest player on the field and the fearless, breathless embodiment of all that Busby wanted for United. The winger darted into the area to meet Roy Keane's first-time cross and glanced home a clinical header. All afternoon, Giggs emancipated his talents, jinking and twisting across the field like a sidewinder. His goal should have marked the opening of the floodgates, but profligate finishing from the Reds and superb goalkeeping from Neville Southall somehow kept the difference narrow.

The woodwork was struck three times, by a deflected Andrei Kanchelskis drive and twice by Eric Cantona, another who revelled in the demands of the occasion. The Frenchman almost provided the afternoon's finishing masterstroke when, while airborne, he chest-controlled a Giggs pass, swivelled and shot in the same motion, only for the ball to bounce away off an upright.

The Frenchman stood, hands on hips, expression aghast, head shaking that the woodwork had dared to blot his masterpiece. Just for one day, however, it didn't matter that the ball had been repelled. This was a day when the genius of Cantona, Giggs and their free-flowing colleagues needed only celebration, not validation.

'He [Sir Matt] would have been pleased with the entertainment, I'm sure of that,' Ferguson grinned afterwards. 'The effort they put in and the commitment was terrific, but he'd have had a rueful old smile and said: "Alex, I've seen it before." The chances we missed in the game were incredible. It would have been nice to get a few more goals but, at the end of the day, the manner in which we played was more important. We tried to play football all the time.'

Indeed they did; football of the finest kind. Football taught by Matt Busby.

## THE TEAMS

**Manchester United:** Schmeichel; Parker, Bruce, Pallister, Irwin; Kanchelskis (McClair 72), Keane, Ince, Giggs; Hughes, Cantona

**Subs not used:** Sealey, Dublin

**Goalscorer:** Giggs 27

**Everton:** Southall; Jackson, Snodin, Moore, Ablett; Warzycha (Hinchcliffe 80), Stuart, Ebbrell, Beagrie; Angell, Cottee (Barlow 46)

**Sub not used:** Kearton

# 13

# MANCHESTER UNITED 1
# FC BARCELONA 0

Champions League semi-final, second leg
29 April 2008
Old Trafford, Manchester

## MAKE BELIEVE

If ever a game defined 'tension', then this was it. Nudged ahead of the free-flowing menace of Barcelona by a majestic strike from Paul Scholes, United squeaked into the 2008 Champions League final in nerve-shredding circumstances.

Perched on their seat edges, 75,061 supporters peeped between fingers as the Reds executed a magnificent rearguard action to deny Frank Rijkaard's incisive side, for whom Lionel Messi – not for the last time – conjured the prospect of doom with his every touch.

Running the full gamut of emotions, a strident home support vocalised their mood throughout, roaring Sir Alex Ferguson's braves forward, bemoaning the excruciating passage of time and whistling as shrilly as a cloud of bats whenever one of Barça's electric-blue nuisances hogged the ball.

The message spelt out in a pre-match mural at the Scoreboard End had urged United's players to 'believe'. Over at the Stretford End, a shimmering silver enlargement of the European Cup, flanked by '68' and '99', clarified the point, in the unlikely event of anyone missing the prize at stake. With the Reds shorn of

Wayne Rooney and Nemanja Vidic by injuries sustained in defeat at Stamford Bridge three days earlier, the call to arms applied just as much to those on the terraces.

A goalless first leg in Camp Nou a week earlier had proven that United could nullify the fluid probing of the Catalans, but Cristiano Ronaldo's early penalty miss hinted that the Reds's chance of a smooth passage to the final in Moscow had passed.

Within the first minute at Old Trafford, it became clear that a long night was in store. Scholes's first contribution was to upend danger-man Messi on the edge of the United area, and time stood still as referee Herbert Fandel assessed the situation before correctly awarding a free-kick rather than a penalty.

There was, however, an explosion of joy to quickly lighten the mood. Gianluca Zambrotta's stray clearance after robbing Ronaldo was a mistake, but scarcely deserved the punishment wielded by Scholes's sledgehammer of a right foot. It seemed that as Barça goalkeeper Victor Valdes moved towards the 25-yard shot, it was swerving further and further away from him. Within a flash, the net was bulging and the crowd erupted.

'That was one I didn't catch quite cleanly,' was Scholes's typically modest recollection of the beautiful moment. 'It seemed to slice off my right foot and, as soon as I hit it, I felt it was in because the keeper seemed to go the other way and there was a massive gap there.'

If ever there was a goal worthy of winning a game of this magnitude, it was this one. Except United had more than three-quarters of the match to still see out – an equaliser by the Catalans would send them through on the away-goals rule.

Nervousness crept into the Reds' play and Messi broke free of the shackles imposed by Patrice Evra and Ji-sung Park to shuffle forward in his inimitable fashion and force Edwin van der Sar into a diving one-handed save. The tireless Park did much to help neutralise the Argentinian's obvious threat, but the Korean also guided a shot inches wide of Valdes's goal after collecting a pass from Ronaldo.

For all the visitors' possession, they were often restricted to efforts from distance, with Wes Brown and Rio Ferdinand patrolling their area diligently. Deco drilled a drive the wrong side of van der Sar's right-hand post and Nani glanced a header fractionally wide to prolong the tension.

Yet the torturous finale inevitably brought some nerve-wracking moments for the home fans to endure. Substitute Thierry Henry, a regular scorer against the Reds in his Arsenal days, headed straight at van der Sar and curled another effort straight at the Dutchman.

Each tackle, interception and hoofed clearance provoked a primal roar of delight, and the scenes of celebration at the final whistle were among the wildest Old Trafford has ever hosted. 'Our fans saw us over the line,' admitted Sir Alex Ferguson. 'We needed a fantastic performance and I think we got one.'

Ferdinand, impressive enough at the back to lead one newspaper to suggest he should be United's Player of the Year ahead of goal-machine Ronaldo, declared: 'We had to dig deep at the end because they put us under pressure. It was our discipline and a moment of quality from a fantastic player that got us through.'

Nine years after missing the Champions League final against

## FAN'S EYE VIEW

'United have a beautiful romance going across India, but I have a superstition of always watching Champions League games alone. So, despite there being several screenings of the Barcelona game around Delhi, I stayed in all day on my own and just kept thinking about the game. I lost count of the prayers I offered! I was so nervous. Even when Scholesy scored, I simply got up from the bed, clenched my fists and quietly retreated to my nervous position. I knew the job wasn't done, and after that it was a classic case of wave after wave of Barça attack and United defended like kings. I don't think I changed my position throughout the second half, and then when the final whistle went I just let my emotions go, screaming and thanking all my Gods.'

Rahul Singh, Delhi, India

Bayern Munich, Scholes had completed his personal redemption by taking the Reds to Moscow. Coming 50 years after the Munich disaster and four decades since the European Cup was first placed in the club's trophy cabinet, the midfielder's intervention merely confirmed Sir Alex's pre-match declaration: 'Fate is fate.' Amid the frenzied post-match celebrations, he and his side had made believers of everyone.

## THE TEAMS

**Manchester United:** van der Sar; Hargreaves, Ferdinand, Brown, Evra (Silvestre 90); Park, Scholes (Fletcher 76), Carrick, Nani (Giggs 76); Ronaldo, Tevez

**Subs not used:** Kuszczak, Anderson, O'Shea, Welbeck

**Goalscorer:** Scholes 14

**Barcelona:** Valdes; Zambrotta, Puyol, Milito, Abidal; Toure (Gudjohnsen 88), Xavi, Deco, Iniesta (Henry 60); Messi, Eto'o (Bojan 72)

**Subs not used:** Pinto, Edmilson, Sylvinho, Thuram

# 12 SL BENFICA 1 MANCHESTER UNITED 5

European Cup quarter-final, second leg
9 March 1966
Estadio da Luz, Lisbon

## EL BEATLE IS BORN

'What a player this boy is,' exclaimed BBC commentator Kenneth Wolstenholme, his pitch steadily climbing, before climaxing with a disbelieving: 'He's got another!' The boy in question, George Best, was familiar to all football followers in Britain. After this demolition of the mighty Benfica, the football world knew his name.

Still only 19, the Ulsterman struck twice as United bagged a flabber-gasting 5-1 victory over Portugal's finest, ending their bid to reach a fifth European Cup final in six years and moving the Reds into a semi-final tie against Partizan Belgrade.

Benfica had escaped Old Trafford with a 3-2 defeat, and were supremely confident of overturning the minor deficit at the famous Estadio da Luz. 'Benfica in 1966 were the cream and had taken over from the legendary Real Madrid as top dogs,' recalled Denis Law. 'Two years previously, we had been beaten five-nil in Lisbon in the Cup-Winners' Cup and, when we went out, all the Portuguese fans were holding their hands with all fingers giving us the salute.'

Mindful that Benfica had never been beaten at home in Europe and were unbeaten in all competitions on their own patch for over nine years, Matt Busby approached the tie cautiously. The strict instructions were to keep matters tight and play pragmatically for the opening half. 'We could ill afford to give away an early goal that would wipe out our slender advantage,' admitted Law.

'To say we were keyed up would be an understatement,' he continued. 'There was an eighty thousand crowd packing the famous Stadium of Light, and I wasn't exactly pleased when Pat Crerand, kicking a ball about in the dressing room, banged it against the mirror. The glass shattered, and though no one said anything, I imagine everyone was thinking about seven years' bad luck. It certainly didn't help the mood.'

Neither did the sight of Eusebio being handed his European Footballer of the Year award moments before kick-off. Unbeknown to all, however, the boy who would succeed the Portuguese superstar just two years later would put the tie out of sight inside the first 15 minutes.

From the first whistle, it became apparent that Best had disregarded his manager's instructions, that both he and John Connelly must sit deep and patrol the wings. 'I couldn't believe it,'

Danny Welbeck sets the ball rolling as he celebrates scoring an early goal against Arsenal in August 2011. A rampant United side bagged another seven goals that day.

Revenge is sweet as United hand out a 5-0 pummelling to local rivals City in November 1994.

Kiko Macheda announces himself to the Old Trafford faithful with a brilliant late goal on his debut to secure victory over Aston Villa and help United on their way to the Premier League title in 2009.

Wayne Rooney joins Chicharito in the celebrations after the Mexican goal-poacher shot United into an early lead against title rivals Chelsea in May 2011. The Reds dominated the battle and won the wider war.

Eric Cantona watches as his stunning volley flies into the net five minutes from time to secure a double Double as Liverpool are beaten in the 1996 FA Cup final.

United pile on the pressure against Athletic Bilbao in the 1957 European Cup quarter-final.

Michael Owen leads the celebrations after scoring the decisive winning goal long into stoppage time in the September 2009 match against City – surely the greatest Manchester derby of all time.

Cristiano Ronaldo slots home the second of his goals to put United 5-0 up against AS Roma in a stunning Champions League quarter-final performance that blew away the Italian opposition.

Bill Foulkes clears the ball after another Real Madrid attack in the 1968 European Cup semi-final. The Munich survivor went on to score the vital goal that put United through to the final.

On a day when everyone remembered Sir Matt Busby, United's latest young prodigy, Ryan Giggs, showed the sort of swagger and skill that the great manager always wanted from his teams.

Paul Scholes thunders home a spectacular goal against Barcelona in the 2008 Champions League semi-final to secure the Reds' passage to Moscow after a game of almost unbearable tension.

A star is born. George Best parades the biggest sombrero he could find after destroying Benfica in the 1966 European Cup quarter-final.

Juan Sebastian Veron takes the congratulations of his team-mates after scoring with a left-foot shot that took United into a 4-3 lead over Spurs in September 2001, having been 3-0 down at half time.

Jack Rowley scores his second goal to equalise against Blackpool in the 1948 FA Cup final. United went on to win 4-2 in one of the best Wembley finals.

Anderlecht goalkeeper Felix Week endures a torrid evening as United run riot at Maine Road, posting a 10-0 club record victory in England's first taster of the European Cup.

Steve Bruce celebrates scoring the winner against Sheffield Wednesday late in added time in April 1993 to ensure that the title was still on.

Shay Brennan scores direct from a corner against Sheffield Wednesday on 19 February 1958, United's first game since the Munich Air Disaster. It was almost as if the fans had willed the ball into the net.

Bryan Robson shakes hands with Diego Maradona of Barcelona ahead of the European Cup-Winners' Cup quarter-final at Old Trafford. The world's greatest player was outshone by 'Captain Marvel', who scored twice in a famous victory.

Munich survivors Matt Busby and Bobby Charlton celebrate a dream fulfilled after United had beaten Benfica 4-1 to win the 1968 European Cup.

Roy Keane scores the first headed goal of his United career against Juventus at the Stadio delle Alpi in the Champions League semi-final of 1999. His all-action performance was one of the outstanding performances in the Irishman's epic career.

Ryan Giggs wheels away in delight after scoring his wonder-goal to decide the FA Cup semi-final replay against Arsenal in April 1999. It was a match that had everything, as the two domestic giants battled it out for supremacy.

The United squad celebrate being crowned champions of Europe for a third time, after a dramatic penalty shoot-out victory over Chelsea in 2008.

Ole Gunnar Solskjaer has just pounced as United complete the most famous late show in the club's history to secure the Champions League title in May 1999.

grinned Busby. 'Out this kid comes as if he's never heard of tradition and starts running at them, turning them inside out. I ought to have shouted at him for not following instructions, but what can you say? He was a law unto himself; he always was.'

It took Best just seven minutes to open the scoring. Tony Dunne's left-wing free-kick was floated towards the penalty spot, and the Northern Irishman sprang to reach it ahead of the onrushing Alberto Costa Pereira before glancing a header into the unguarded goal. Almost immediately, he struck again, only to have his prodded finish ruled out for a perceived offside. In fact, he had been a yard onside.

No matter. Best responded by serving up the goal of the night. David Herd nodded Harry Gregg's long punt down to the teenager, 40 yards from goal. He needed only two touches to surge away from three defenders and into the Benfica area, where he cracked a low shot through Pereira's legs to all but end the tie. United's players, never prone to overt celebrations, leapt around in a bouncing hub of joy. Nobody quite knew how to behave – this was uncharted territory, after all – and when Best released Connelly to poke home United's third goal, Law's reaction was to smash the ball back into the net, then beat the ground in the manner of some vexed ape.

Benfica had never before conceded more than two goals at home in Europe. Quarter of an hour in, United had three. No wonder all decorum had gone out of the window. 'Easy, easy, easy' mocked the small (and evidently brave) band of away supporters.

The teeming masses of home supporters were stunned and grew increasingly tetchy as the game wore on. When Eusebio guided a 25-yard free-kick against the base of Gregg's post, they barely raised a murmur, though they did muster a roar of delight when Shay Brennan followed half time with a spectacular own-goal, lobbed gently but accurately over Gregg and inside the far post.

A comeback never appeared a realistic possibility, however, and it was United who always carried the greater menace on the counter-attack, even if Best was occasionally guilty of overplaying matters. But, as Bobby Charlton later put it: 'How the hell do you shout at someone who's just announced he's a genius?'

It was one of the visitors' unsung heroes, Crerand, who would land the next telling blow. Law picked out his fellow Scot's uncharacteristically rampaging run into space and, as goalkeeper Pereira allowed himself to lose his bearings, Crerand hooked a finish back across him and into the untended goal.

Game over, yet United were insatiable for the remainder of the game. Another delightful team move yielded a sparkling fifth goal that illuminated the Estadio da Luz, as Best meandered infield and fed Herd, who adroitly teed up the onrushing Charlton. Rather than spank home a trademark howitzer, however, he simply glided past Pereira and tapped home a finish that embodied the lucidity of United's collective display. 'What a super goal,' purred Wolstenholme. 'That is the pink ribbon on this luscious box of chocolates that Manchester United have given us tonight.'

Benfica fans were less charitable by this point. Their newfound hobby of hurling the cushions from their seats at any United player who approached touch may have been harmless enough, but the final whistle prompted a sinister turn of events as both sets of supporters cascaded onto the field; the few hundred away fans were in jubilant mood, but their humiliated home counterparts made straight for the United players to vent their fury. Ugly scenes followed in which several punches were thrown and Charlton's shirt was torn from his back, but nothing could top the result for shock value.

'It was incredible,' admitted Law, 'and the best performance in my view of a United team in Europe, especially as we beat them on their own patch. It was a beautiful experience and a joy to share in that splendid team effort.'

While the collective effort and savvy on show had done for Benfica, there was no question who had stolen the limelight. 'I wasn't in awe but I did know that I was ready,' recalled Best. 'That, whatever the outcome of the game, this was the sort of stage I was meant to play on. It was perfect theatre. On nights like that, good players become great players and great players become gods.'

The following morning, as Best was being photographed sporting a huge sombrero at Manchester Airport, the Portuguese media eulogised about the boy wonder who had savaged their champions. No longer was George Best a secret weapon; he was now, after translation, 'the fifth Beatle'.

## THE TEAMS

**SL Benfica:** Costa Pereira; Pinto, Germano, Silva; Cavem, Cruz; Coluna, Eusebio; Augusto, Torres, Simoes

**Goalscorer:** Brennan 52 (og)

**Manchester United:** Gregg; Dunne, Foulkes, Brennan; Connelly, Stiles, Crerand, Best; Herd, Charlton, Law

**Goalscorers:** Best 7, 12, Connelly 14, Crerand 78, Charlton 84

# 11

## TOTTENHAM HOTSPUR 3
## MANCHESTER UNITED 5

**Premier League**
**12 September 2001**
**White Hart Lane, London**

# UNITED'S GREATEST-EVER
# PREMIER LEAGUE COMEBACK

The archetypal 'game of two halves' panned out in the most dramatic fashion at a sun-soaked White Hart Lane as the champions produced a Jekyll and Hyde performance in the capital.

United came into the game on the back of a disappointing defeat against Deportivo La Coruna in the Champions League, which had prompted criticism from all quarters and raised questions about the overall quality of the expensively assembled side stuttering in its pursuit of a fourth straight Premier League title.

Suffering a Spanish hangover, the Reds were simply abject for the first 45 minutes, but untouchable thereafter as Sir Alex Ferguson's side thrived on having the odds stacked against them. For the opening period, they even seemed intent on making hard work for themselves; conceding sloppy goals with feckless regularity.

Tottenham debutant Dean Richards powered home an early header from a Christian Ziege corner, before Gustavo Poyet's pass sprung a ramshackle offside trap and Les Ferdinand drilled a clinical finish past the exposed Fabien Barthez.

When an unmarked Ziege nodded home at the back post in first-half injury-time, United looked in total disarray. David Beckham and Gary Neville started an animated inquest into the defending that had allowed the German so much freedom when Poyet supplied the cross, but the mood in White Hart Lane's away dressing room was, in fact, substantially calmer.

Beckham, skipper in the absence of the suspended Roy Keane, revealed: 'Everyone knows I am a quiet captain so I wasn't the one doing the shouting at half time. The manager was quite relaxed, believe it or not. He had a few words with every one of us because none of us were playing well. We just needed to sort ourselves out.'

The home support cranked up the crowing during the interval – and it continued behind the scenes. 'At half time Spurs were gloating as if they were going to come out and beat us by five,' recalls Andy Cole. 'We had other ideas.'

Quite so. Cole's diving header from Neville's cross reduced the arrears within a minute of the restart, spiking United's dander and setting jitters loose in the stands. Over in the Park Lane end, the travelling Reds responded by ratcheting up the volume. The half-time introduction of Mikael Silvestre for Denis Irwin gave United greater attacking verve down the left flank, while Ole Gunnar Solskjaer's replacement at the expense of Nicky Butt, who sustained a rib injury, offered further menace for Glenn Hoddle's three-man defence to consider.

## WHAT THE PAPERS SAID

"A hat-trick of headers in the space of 25 minutes cancelled out the three-goal lead Tottenham had established in a pinch-yourself first half, and the conclusive act of a shake-your-head second was the low drive from Veron that had all but assured United of all three points before Beckham shot past Sullivan with sweet resonance."

Patrick Barclay, *The Times*

Goalkeeper Neil Sullivan found his goal increasingly under siege, and was beaten just before the hour when Laurent Blanc rose – unmarked – to power home Beckham's corner for his one and only Premier League goal. The timing was impeccable. Tottenham's play was gripped with fear of the inevitable, while United's was galvanised by the prospect of it.

Ruud van Nistelrooy latched onto a fine Silvestre cross to nod the Reds level with 18 minutes remaining, his fifth strike since joining in the summer, and there was only ever

going to be one winner. 'All eleven of us players, and our fans, believed we would do it,' stressed the deadly Dutchman. 'So when I scored for 3-3, that wasn't enough for us. We knew it was there for us to win it.'

Juan Sebastian Veron then stylishly capped one of his finest domestic displays for the Reds by powering forward to edge the visitors in front. The Argentine had pulled all the strings in United's fightback, and stepped forward to completely overturn the scoreline, following snappy passes by Paul Scholes and Solskjaer, when he drove a low, left-footed effort inside Sullivan's left-hand post from just inside the box.

Cue pandemonium amid jubilant, writhing supporters off the field and a grinning pile of Red-clad euphoria on it, as Veron slid towards the corner flag, while the staff on the United bench simply afforded themselves knowing smiles.

They only broke into full, contented grins when Solskjaer weaved his way down the left flank and pulled the ball back invitingly for Beckham to chest down and drill home the killer fifth goal with unerring accuracy past Sullivan, the same man he had beaten from considerably further out during the keeper's Wimbledon days.

There was inevitable debate as to quite how United had emerged for the second half looking a completely different side to the one that was so off key for the opening 45 minutes. How had the manager managed to orchestrate a scarcely believable turn of events, particularly if he'd resisted the urge to dish out the infamous 'hairdryer' treatment?

The man himself was quick to pay

tribute to the influence of his Norwegian substitute Solskjaer, rather than take credit for any half-time words of wisdom: 'He was the key with his runs and movement. He was magnificent and gave Silvestre the space to run into.' It was the opposite flank, however, which Spurs stopper Richards cited as the visitors' route back into the game.

'Neville and Beckham were both demanding the ball,' stated the defender. 'Gary seemed to be attacking and attacking all the time. Gary pushed forward in support of David and made the overlaps which caused us all the problems.'

Whichever route United took to a sporting miracle, its resonance was immediately apparent to Sir Alex who, at the time looking forward to his mooted 2002 retirement, admitted: 'I'll look back on days like this and it will be fantastic.' While the manager ultimately postponed his departure for over another decade, his sentiment still rings true.

In isolation, the thrilling victory may have been a performance worthy of only three points in a season that ultimately ended with United in third place, 10 points behind champions Arsenal, yet its significance is far greater for all supporters. This was the proof that no match is ever irretrievable for any of Sir Alex's teams. Stack the odds as high as you like; Manchester United are always capable of finding a way over them.

## THE TEAMS

**Tottenham Hotspur:** Sullivan; Taricco, Richards, Perry; Anderton (Rebrov 83), Poyet, Freund, Sherwood, Ziege; Sheringham, Ferdinand

**Subs not used:** Keller, Etherington, Davies, Thelwell

**Goalscorers:** Richards 10, Ferdinand 25, Ziege 45

**Manchester United:** Barthez; G. Neville, Johnsen, Blanc, Irwin (Silvestre 46); Beckham, Butt (Solskjaer 40), Veron, Scholes; Cole, van Nistelrooy

**Subs not used:** Carroll, P. Neville, Chadwick

**Goalscorers:** Cole 46, Blanc 57, van Nistelrooy 71, Veron 75, Beckham 86

# 10 MANCHESTER UNITED 4 BLACKPOOL 2

FA Cup final
24 April 1948
Wembley Stadium, London

## BLACKPOOL ROCKED

United's first-ever match at Wembley not only thrust the club into the spotlight against a Blackpool side containing England favourites Stanley Matthews and Stan Mortensen, it also allowed Matt Busby's men to put on the kind of entertainment that would become synonymous with the Reds over subsequent years.

Trailing at half time, United displayed the greater stamina and conviction towards the end of a compelling encounter that thrilled not only those present at the famous stadium but those following events from far beyond. A classic unfolded in the April sunshine on a bowling green of a pitch and, in truth, the result could have gone either way in a showpiece that continues to be regarded as one of the seminal FA Cup finals.

Nearly 100,000 fans jostled to watch the action as both teams played in a changed strip – United in blue and Blackpool in white and black – but the identity of the clubs

remained very much intact. Busby's tactics to nullify the substantial threat of wing wizard Matthews worked to a tee. This enabled his own team to play the attractive passing game that had accounted for top-flight opponents all along the road to Wembley, despite being forced to play 'home' matches away from Old Trafford due to bomb damage sustained in World War II.

Jack Crompton had to overcome the agony of having an abscess on his spine lanced in order to take his place in goal in front of the watching King George VI, and the United stopper became a central figure in the drama. 'I knew whatever pain my back was going to give me had to be endured for the good of the team and the supporters, who were depending on us to win the cup,' he recalled.

The keeper had no chance with the opening goal, which arrived in controversial circumstances. Allenby Chilton's lunging foul on Mortensen should have resulted in only a free-kick, even if it would have been deemed worthy of a red card in today's game. 'While I did trip Stan, I felt sure it was outside the area,' protested Chilton, who was tested by Mortensen's power throughout. Referee Jack Barrick pointed to the spot and Eddie Shimwell blasted in the penalty. 'I'm glad the goal didn't decide the match,' added Chilton.

The bar denied Henry Cockburn an equaliser, but United did draw level when Jack Rowley cleverly looped the ball over the advancing Joe Robinson and almost arrogantly converted a confident finish, after Eric Hayward made a hash of Jimmy Delaney's through-ball. Delaney, who had already lifted the Scottish Cup with Celtic, should not have played due to a cracked bone in his right leg. 'It troubled me,' he confessed. 'But this was one time you just had to keep on going.'

Back came the Seasiders with danger-man Mortensen, who scored in every round of the competition, firing in off the far post from a tight angle after a Matthews free-kick was helped on by Hugh Kelly. Undeterred, Busby instructed his troops at half time: 'Play football. Take your chances. If you lose, then lose by playing football.'

Yet United needed to remain patient and could easily have fallen further behind. John Aston had to shepherd the ball behind the goal when Mortensen challenged Crompton, as the Tangerines' plan to hit long balls through to the centre-forward threatened to bear fruit.

Instead, the scores were level again with 20 minutes remaining. Johnny Morris's quick free-kick allowed Rowley to leap prodigiously and despatch a glorious header past Robinson. 'It was one of the most magnificent goals I have ever seen,' wrote journalist Alan Hoby. 'Just as this was one of the best finals I shall ever report.'

## WHAT THE PAPERS SAID

'Now I have seen it all. I shall never forget this final. Nor shall I forget the still, spread-eagled figure of Manchester's man of destiny – Jack Rowley – his shirt a blue stain on that brilliant green turf, after he had headed the goal which put United level for the second time in this blistering battle. For Rowley shattered Blackpool as surely as an iron heel crushing a China doll. Against any other team in Britain, Blackpool would have won the cup. But when Rowley leapt galvanically into the air to that "impossible" chance, all their pretensions and illusions were stripped from them.'

Alan Hoby, *People*

Rowley enthused: 'I just had to get that ball in. I knew a goal then meant so much to us. When I realised I had equalised, it was the happiest moment of my life.'

The threat posed by Matthews was largely stifled by Aston and Charlie Mitten, who tracked back and made a number of key tackles, but Mortensen remained a menace and forced a great stop out of Crompton that proved crucial. The keeper's subsequent throw launched a retaliatory raid through John Anderson from which Stan Pearson, who scored a hat-trick at Hillsborough in the semi-final against Derby County, edged his team in front for the first time.

Former Salford schoolboy Pearson had to expertly work his way past defender Hayward to shoot but realised this was his moment of glory. 'I felt helpless out there as I watched Mortensen go through,' he said. 'Then, suddenly, I found the ball at my feet. Crompton's clearance was passed to me by Anderson and I saw my chance.'

Two minutes later, Anderson unleashed a long-range drive that took a deflection via Kelly and crashed in off the underside of the bar to emphatically put the seal on a famous victory.

Captain Johnny Carey, quiet by his own high standards, dropped the lid of the trophy on the pitch after receiving it from the king but was otherwise unflustered by events, remarking: 'I felt our good soccer was bound to win it.'

In keeping with a sportingly contested final, Mortensen, unlucky to miss out on a winner's medal, visited the United dressing room to offer his congratulations. 'I was sorry Stan had to be on the losing side for he's a great player,' admitted Chilton. United were similarly even-handed; Delaney, whose injury had been kept quiet all week, also still found the time to pass on advice to a nervous Johnny Crosland after hearing of his marker's shock inclusion in the Blackpool line-up ahead of kick-off. The part-timer, who played at left-back, headed dramatically away from under his own bar at one stage and must have appreciated the pre-match support.

But for all the camaraderie and spirit between two rival teams, it was the sporting feast fit for a king that most enthralled the nation. Busby's team would finish runners-up in the league for a third successive season the following year, but untold riches of silverware and acclaim would follow as his sound footballing principles began to reap dividends.

## THE TEAMS

**Manchester United:** Crompton; Carey, Aston; Anderson, Chilton, Cockburn; Delaney, Morris, Rowley, Pearson, Mitten

**Goalscorers:** Rowley 28, 70, Pearson 80, Anderson 82

**Blackpool:** Robinson; Shimwell, Crosland; Johnston, Hayward, Kelly; Matthews, Munro, Mortensen, Dick, Rickett

**Goalscorers:** Shimwell 12 (pen), Mortensen 35

# 9 MANCHESTER UNITED 10 ANDERLECHT 0

European Cup preliminary round, second leg
26 September 1956
Maine Road, Manchester

## RECORD BREAKERS

United sent shockwaves through Europe with an astonishing annihilation of Anderlecht as English football hosted its first competitive continental encounter. The goals flowed as freely as the pouring rain as the Reds notched an incredible ten-goal victory over the Belgian champions.

Managed by an Englishman, Bill Gormlie, the visitors had provided a test in the first leg, but slipped to a 2-0 defeat after Martin Lippens missed a penalty. 'This was no little team from Malta or Iceland,' contended Matt Busby. 'Belgium was a strong soccer nation and Anderlecht were its champions.' Indeed, the Mauves had won the title for three years in succession and defeated Arsenal on their previous visit to England – a prestigious friendly at Highbury in October 1953.

While the construction of Old Trafford's floodlights continued, a comparatively meagre gate of 43,635 fans – dwarfed by later attendances against Borussia Dortmund and

Athletic Bilbao – flocked to Maine Road intrigued by the prospect of witnessing European Cup action for the first time. There was a fascination about the competition – 'one that combines some of the thrill of our own FA Cup with a dash of continental flavour,' according to one newspaper report – but the Belgians must have soon wondered if it was a wasted trip.

After a lengthy journey to the north of England, they were tormented in the Maine Road mud and left chasing shadows, with any thoughts of retrieving a two-goal deficit from the first leg soon turning to a matter of mere damage limitation, even if their attempts to keep passing the ball showed a determination to stick to manager Gormlie's principles.

Yet United's own passing game was light years ahead of the time, and Busby's tactics were far superior. There was an electricity and fluency in the Babes' play that turned a tentative step into the unknown into a turkey shoot, as the Scot's initial fear that the tie was still in the balance on a rain-soaked surface soon vanished.

The opener after eight minutes set the tone for the evening as Roger Byrne's volleyed clearance allowed the lively David Pegg to fly down the wing past two defenders and centre for Tommy Taylor to bullet a downward header into the net. The quality of the goal was exceptional, but it proved only a taster for the feast of football that followed.

With Duncan Edwards – introduced for Jackie Blanchflower in the only change from the Brussels encounter – and Eddie Colman in imperious form at wing-half, a stranglehold was achieved on the game and strapping centre-forward Taylor doubled his personal tally on 20 minutes by toe-punting home following a short corner.

Four minutes later, Felix Week was left exposed by some sloppy defending and Dennis Viollet rounded the keeper to profit, before then intercepting a terrible back-header to blast in for a double. Defenders Wim De Koster and Jacques Culot hardly covered themselves in glory during those incidents, but the punishment was nonetheless ruthless.

Viollet was celebrating a hat-trick seconds later, after a flowing move involving half of the team, rounding it off with a left-footed drive into the top corner from the edge of the box.

'From Anderlecht's point of view, the floodlights might just as well not have been on,' wrote one correspondent. 'They were utterly in the dark.'

## WHAT THE PAPERS SAID

'All very well, it may be argued, but where was the opposition? Apparently not at Maine Road. And yet this should not entirely detract from the merit of United's performance. There is a pitch of excellence which is absolute irrespective of the circumstances in which it is reached and United certainly had it this evening.'

An Old International, *Guardian*

Any thoughts that United would ease off in the second half were dismissed when Taylor capitalised on more confusion inside the Anderlecht box to ram in for his hat-trick, and the punishment kept on coming for the bewildered and bedraggled Belgians.

Billy Whelan got in on the act after earlier being thwarted by a magnificent stop by the shell-shocked Week. Byrne was involved in the build-up and the captain ventured forward again to supply the most inviting of crosses for Viollet to plunder number eight, with his fourth of a productive night.

With an average age of 22, the infectious enthusiasm of youth was married to a competitive edge. With the floodgates well and truly open, the youngsters continued to move in for the kill – even if Anderlecht's sportsmanship and character in the face of such a drubbing drew widespread praise afterwards.

Johnny Berry had been hunting a strike of his own and, when he found the net, only Pegg was missing from the forwards in terms of getting on the scoresheet. Try as they might, his team-mates were unable to tee up a goal for the outstanding outside-left who switched flanks and ran the defence ragged. Double figures were still reached, courtesy of Whelan, following fine work by Berry with barely a minute left on the clock.

The scoreline remains a club record victory for United. Busby was unequivocal in his assessment when reflecting on the most memorable of evenings: 'I have just got to say that we ran up what has to be regarded in football circles as a cricket score because we played darned well! I was becoming accustomed to see the great team of those days playing

well, but they excelled themselves that night. It was, in fact, the finest exhibition of teamwork I had ever seen from any side either at club or international level.'

If further independent analysis is needed to gauge the true level of the football on show, referee Mervyn Griffiths was able to offer his opinion after getting a first-hand view of the bewitching performance. 'United were absolutely awesome,' he enthused. 'I have refereed teams all over Europe but I have never seen football like United displayed and the precision of their passing was remarkable. Even after they had scored the tenth goal, they were still running as if the game had only just started.'

The display highlighted the desire of Busby and his players to conquer the continent after proving to be top dogs in England. The story of United in the European Cup had enjoyed an incredible opening, but the lurking tragedy of Munich would ultimately deprive this band of remarkable players of the chance to lift the trophy.

Their aim would be realised, however, by future iterations of United, all of whom owed a debt of discovery to their famed forebears. The highs of 1968, 1999 and 2008 all had their roots in this rampage in the rain at Maine Road when United made the biggest of splashes in the brave new world of European competition.

## THE TEAMS

**Manchester United:** Wood; Byrne, Foulkes; Edwards, Jones, Colman; Berry, Whelan, Taylor, Viollet, Pegg

**Goalscorers:** Taylor 8, 20, 54, Viollet 26, 39, 40, 75, Whelan 63, 89, Berry 78

**Anderlecht:** Week; Gettemans, Culot; Hanon, de Koster, van der Wilt; De Drijver, Van den Bosch, Mermans, Dewael, Jurion

# 8 MANCHESTER UNITED 2
# SHEFFIELD WEDNESDAY 1

Premier League
10 April 1993
Old Trafford, Manchester

## BACK FROM THE DEAD

'Every United fan I speak to shakes my hand and says: "Sheffield Wednesday, 10 April 1993 at ten to five, thank you for those two goals,"' smiles Steve Bruce, hero of the afternoon when United finally smashed their title neurosis to end a 26-year wait for domestic rule. 'We were dead and gone. Suddenly you get your head to a couple and they fly in. It was fabulous.'

A year after imploding amid a sapping run of fixture congestion to hand the First Division title to Leeds United, the Reds were once again apparently teetering on the brink of collapse in a tit-for-tat race with Aston Villa, having won just once in five games and trailing the Villans by a point.

Losing to Trevor Francis's Wednesday with four minutes of normal time remaining, only the giddiest optimist could have conceived that the Reds would prise a victory from the jaws of defeat. Enter

Bruce, with a pair of clinically taken headers to spark frenzied celebrations that would resonate over the coming decades of success.

Each Premier League title triumph stemmed from the first back in 1992-93, and Alex Ferguson was in no doubt of the importance of Bruce's intervention. 'The nail in Villa's coffin, no question, was our late, late show against Sheffield Wednesday,' he beamed.

An afternoon of nerve-shredding drama had begun in apparently routine fashion. Wednesday, chasing UEFA Cup qualification, were indebted to the efforts of goalkeeper Chris Woods. The England stopper repelled a succession of early efforts, most notably from Mark Hughes and Brian McClair. Yet, as would become customary, United eschewed the easy route to victory in favour of picking their way across the precipice of doom.

Referee Michael Peck suffered a

hamstring injury after an hour, prompting a stoppage in play and the entrance of senior linesman John Hilditch as the new man in the middle. His first deed of note was to award a penalty against Paul Ince for a lunging challenge on Chris Waddle. Though the United midfielder paraded indignity at the call, Hilditch had no choice and Stretford-born John Sheridan calmly rolled the penalty past Peter Schmeichel.

Alex Ferguson's response was swift. United's tempo had dropped after a strong opening, and the players' collective body language betrayed their sense of impending doom, so on went club captain Bryan Robson. 'I had to bring him on,' the manager later conceded. 'He brought a sense of purpose to us, a sense of nerve, too.'

The move met widespread praise, not least from the *Daily Express*, whose report exclaimed: 'Bryan Robson reappeared like a consultant surgeon waving his tray of instruments. A scalpel here and a stitch there and United, looking dead and gone, were suddenly leaping the theatre.'

United's Eastertime resurrection began with more regular examinations of Woods, who continued to clutch, parry or stop the ball whenever it came remotely in his vicinity. The Reds were still trailing when it became apparent that Villa had stuttered to a goalless draw at home to Coventry. It was a decent result for United, but still an extra step closer to the title for Ron Atkinson's side as things stood.

## WHAT THE PAPERS SAID

'What one day brings, another can take away. But if ever there was an afternoon when the championship seemed destined finally to return to Old Trafford, then this was it. As time slipped away and Wednesday clung to a 1-0 lead, the shadows of the West Stand's cantilever roof, nearing completion, were strung out like the bars of a prison across the area of pitch United were attacking. United having served 26 years since their last league title, there were unbearable intimations of another 12 months banged up with fading pin-ups of Best, Law and Charlton. Then along came Steve Bruce, a latter-day Billy Foulkes. If it is true that a hero is no more exceptional than an ordinary man but is exceptional for five or six minutes longer, then the United defender fitted the bill to perfection.'

Stephen Bierley, *Guardian*

'They must have been soaking in the bath at Villa Park,' recalled Ferguson, 'soothing muscles with the knowledge that Wednesday had us in trouble.' Over the next ten minutes, however, United would pull the plug on Villa's momentum.

Bruce, a solid performer all

afternoon, met Denis Irwin's out-swinging corner 15 yards out, straining every sinew to somehow redirect his header over the stretching Woods – and the inexplicably static Nigel Worthington, leaning on the post seemingly without a care in the world – and hauled United level.

It was a captain's contribution, but one which would be topped in staggering circumstances. Popular myth decrees that referee Hilditch merely kept playing until United scored the winner, and Wednesday manager Francis quipped: 'They needed extra-time to beat us.' In fact, play was stopped for almost four minutes for the change of official, while time was also accrued through injuries to Schmeichel, Bruce, Sheridan, Viv Anderson and Carlton Palmer. The manager, who studied the tape post-match, claimed 12 minutes should have been added: 'The referee actually short-changed us – we should have played for at

least four minutes longer than we did.'

As it transpired, just eight minutes were played, only six were needed. Both teams decamped to the Wednesday half until, in the defining act of a season and a generation, Bruce struck again. Ryan Giggs's cross found its way to Gary Pallister, in an unlikely moonlighting stint on the right wing, and the defender's deflected cross looped and dipped perfectly for Bruce to steamroller his way through a packed area, power a header past Woods and set Old Trafford aflame with joy.

'I went berserk, the boss went semi-berserk,' smiled assistant manager Brian Kidd, who jumped into club folklore with a skywards leap and fist-clenching salute to the heavens on the Old Trafford turf. Referee Hilditch duly brought proceedings to a close. 'He might just as well have tootled on a victory trumpet as well because that single result was so decisive in winning the championship,' claimed Ferguson.

In fact, United were only a point ahead with five games remaining. From that quintet, the Reds took 15 points to Villa's six and ended up finishing ten points clear. Bruce's brace provided the unquestioned tipping point for that success, and provided the root from which the modern United's penchant for procuring last-gasp victories grew.

## THE TEAMS

**Manchester United:** Schmeichel; Parker (Robson 68), Bruce, Pallister, Irwin; Sharpe, Ince, McClair, Giggs; Cantona, Hughes

**Subs not used:** Sealey, Phelan

**Goalscorer:** Bruce 86, 90+6

**Sheffield Wednesday:** Woods; Nilsson, Worthington, Anderson, King; Wilson (Bart-Williams 60), Palmer, Sheridan, Waddle; Jemson (Bright 53), Watson

**Subs not used:** Pressman

**Goalscorer:** Sheridan 64 (pen)

# 7 MANCHESTER UNITED 3
# SHEFFIELD WEDNESDAY 0

**FA Cup fifth round**
**19 February 1958**
**Old Trafford, Manchester**

# UNITED WILL GO ON ...

Less than a fortnight after the horror of Munich, United took their first, tottering steps along the road to recovery amid incredible scenes at Old Trafford.

On a night when 11 blank spaces famously comprised the home line-up in the *United Review*, a makeshift side managed by Jimmy Murphy overcame Sheffield Wednesday to reach the FA Cup quarter-finals. A club in tatters, a team decimated and a manager lying stricken. That United were able to fulfil the fixture was incredible; to win it bordered on the stupefying.

With Matt Busby still hospitalised in Munich, assistant manager Murphy took the reins and desperately sought to pull together a team. Instantly promoting a host of players from the club's reserve and youth teams, Murphy also took advantage of the Football Association's benevolent decision to relax its rule on fielding cup-tied

players by signing Blackpool's Ernie Taylor.

'No one realises I went through hell and back and I had no one to talk to, really,' the Welshman admitted. 'Plenty of people were around, but I'm talking about at my level in soccer. I had to find a team of eleven to play. We didn't know what the team would be.'

Such uncertainty remained virtually until kick-off. Murphy whisked his side away to Blackpool to prepare for the game, and he was still finalising his squad with less than two hours to go until the game.

The line-up was completed by Stan Crowther, who started the day on Aston Villa's books, made the trip to Old Trafford with his manager Eric Houghton and was told to join United. Upon protesting that he didn't even have boots, Crowther was amazed when Houghton produced the wing-half's boots from a carrier bag. He signed 75 minutes before kick-off, and again benefited from the FA overlooking a previous Cup outing for the Villans.

Crowther joined his new team-mates in the home dressing room, where there was an inevitably eerie mood among those changing for battle. 'I couldn't get Roger [Byrne] out of my mind,' recalled Ian Greaves. 'I was getting changed where he would have sat. I was wearing his shirt.'

Despite the sombre air, club chairman Harold Hardman spoke defiantly of his club's strength and resolve. The programme's front cover was headlined: 'United will go on ...' before Hardman wrote: 'Although we mourn our dead and grieve for our wounded, we believe that great days are not done for us. The sympathy and encouragement of the football world and particularly of our supporters will justify and inspire us. The road back may be long and hard but, with the memory of those who died at Munich, of their stirring achievements and wonderful sportsmanship ever with us, Manchester United will rise again.'

Despite the rousing tone of Hardman's written address, the pre-match volume in the stands seldom rose above a restrained hum. Almost 60,000 supporters, many of them sporting black armbands, crammed onto the terraces, while several thousand more were locked outside and remained there throughout the game, in the hope that one of the plentiful touts – some charging ten times the face value of a ticket – would come up trumps.

## WHAT THE PAPERS SAID

'Behind that simple catalogue of fact – Manchester United 3, Sheffield Wednesday 0 – lies a football legend that will never be forgotten. This was a makeshift team put out hopefully, anxiously, in an attempt to patch up the team so tragically wrecked in Munich. There was no sympathy from Sheffield Wednesday. They gave this patched-up team the courtesy and tribute of playing as hard as any 11 players could. They were beaten because this Manchester United team were far too good for them. They were beaten for skill, for strength, and for team-work. Players who had never played together blended into a glorious whole and presented a team show I shall never forget.'

Desmond Hackett, *Daily Express*

For those fortunate enough to make it inside, what unfolded was a once-in-a-lifetime experience. The *Guardian*'s W.R.Taylor wrote: 'After one minute's silence, which had a background like the murmur of the sea, United were given a rapturous reception. Each name as it was announced was cheered resoundingly. Bill Foulkes, who had been appointed captain, probably received the loudest and he, as a reward to the crowd for its faith in him, won the toss. A roar greeted every United move, a scream every threat. Sheffield Wednesday must have thought they were playing about 60,000 people – and they were not far wrong.'

It was another Munich survivor – goalkeeper Harry Gregg – who kept the show together early on as Wednesday enjoyed the better of the play. Then, almost from nothing, United broke the deadlock. Debutant Shay Brennan, a full-back by trade but operating as a winger, curled in a left-wing corner which Wednesday goalkeeper Brian Ryalls totally misjudged and merely helped on its way into the net.

'The Old Trafford stands nearly disintegrated,' noted *Guardian* scribe Taylor. Hats and scarves were sent skywards through the industrial smoke of Trafford Park, flung in cathartic, joyous relief that, after a

hellish fortnight, Manchester United were indeed still there.

The pepped-up efforts of Gregg, who produced a string of fine saves, ensured that the Reds would take their lead into the interval, but he was not the only hero. Foulkes revelled in his role as captain, all-action central defender Ronnie Cope charged into challenge after challenge, veteran new boy Taylor bewitched and beguiled the Wednesday defenders and Alex Dawson was menacingly sharp at the cutting edge of the attack.

United's pressure steadily built until, with 20 minutes remaining, Brennan added another chapter to his personal fairytale with a second goal. Mark Pearson chanced his arm from just outside the area but, while Ryalls's knee kept out the initial effort, the rebound fell for Brennan to take a touch and fire home.

Again, cue bedlam. 'Everyone who was within two miles of this ground who was not stone deaf must have known about it,' remarked *Daily Express* writer Desmond Hackett. Yet still the volume steadily rose, reaching an almighty crescendo five minutes from time as Pearson wound his way down the right flank and pulled the ball back for Dawson to thunder home a fine finish.

'Then came the final whistle,' concluded one report. 'The crowd moved like a sea under the floodlights, shaking with their own cheers. They will almost have heard them in Munich.'

There, at Rechts der Isar Hospital, the less seriously injured survivors of the disaster, including Bobby Charlton, listened to radio updates from Old Trafford and telephoned their congratulations to 'Murphy's Marvels'. Unaware of events, however, was Matt Busby. Staff and patients were forbidden from mentioning the game to him, lest they prompt further questions about the crash, as Busby was still unaware of the full fate of his squad.

His recuperation came first, reasoned the doctors. Busby knew that his club was in safe hands with Jimmy Murphy, and the Welshman had assembled a ragtag squad that boasted little reputation, but shared a surfeit of heart and soul to convince any onlooker that they were true United players.

As centre-half Cope would later describe: 'We'd lost some of the best players – the greatest players – but we hadn't lost the spirit: that was what carried us through.'

## THE TEAMS

**Manchester United:** Gregg; Foulkes, Cope; Crowther, Goodwin, Greaves; Pearson, Taylor, Dawson, Webster, Brennan

**Goalscorers:** Brennan 29, 70, Dawson 84

**Sheffield Wednesday:** Ryalls; Martin, Johnson; Kay, Swan, O'Donnell; Wilkinson, Quixall, Baker, Froggatt, Cargill

# 6

## MANCHESTER UNITED 3
## FC BARCELONA 0

European Cup-Winners' Cup quarter-final,
second leg
21 March 1984
Old Trafford, Manchester

# MARVEL HERO

Universally acknowledged as one of Old Trafford's noisiest nights, the Theatre of Dreams became a cauldron of frenzied excitement to inspire Ron Atkinson's side to a remarkable second-leg turnaround against a star-studded Barcelona side.

The Catalans were 2-0 up from the first leg and contained world-class talents Diego Maradona and Bernd Schuster in their ranks, but this tie was all about Reds skipper Bryan Robson. The midfielder was thought to be on the brink of joining Juventus at the time, but was a man with a point to prove after feeling personally responsible for the first-leg deficit.

The United midfielder admits he 'switched off perhaps for the only time in my career' when thinking he was offside at Camp Nou and missed a simple chance. 'I knew I had to make up for my mistakes and thankfully I did,' he declared.

Maradona may have been rated only 70 per cent fit, Schuster revealing the Argentinian had been virtually dragged out of his sick-bed, but even at his brilliant best he'd have struggled to resist the pressing and harassing of a United team playing like men possessed.

Seeds of doubt were sown in Barça minds when Javier 'Urruti' Urruticoechea looked less than confident when coming off his line to attempt to meet a Ray Wilkins centre. Alesanco beat him to it and Norman Whiteside, who missed the first game through injury, saw his lob eventually drop out of the sky and land on top of the bar.

Gary Bailey certainly detected vulnerability in his opposite number. 'The crowd were so fired up, I think it unnerved the Barcelona keeper who dropped one or two balls,' he recalled. 'The crowd was so intimidating and piled so much pressure on him, he just couldn't cope.'

With edginess spreading

throughout the opposition defence, Arthur Albiston's run down the left allowed Wilkins to plant a corner into the danger zone. Graeme Hogg, who put through his own net in Spain, flicked on for Robson to head horizontally into the net from close range.

Returning from the break with renewed optimism, the players responded to the Stretford End's prompting and hounded the Catalans incessantly. 'It's not that they didn't fancy it, but they were looking over their shoulders,' admitted Wilkins. 'We just kept hammering at them. Eventually, the door broke down.'

Victor Munoz was rushed into a reckless, blind back-pass that forced Urruti to tackle the eager Whiteside. The typically tigerish Remi Moses retrieved the situation to cross for Wilkins and, when Urruti made an awful hash of his save, Robson pounced on the loose ball with relish.

'On a night like this, you have to ask how dare United consider selling this man,' questioned commentator Martin Tyler. Swarming all over the yellow shirts, the Reds quickly regained possession and Robson swung the ball wide with the outside of his right boot.

Such was the urgency in the hosts' ranks, Albiston had to fight off Arnold Muhren to receive the pass and the crowd, sensing instant gratification, were cheering as the accurate cross worked its way to the back post. Whiteside climbed to get

in a header that provoked another roar, but it needed Frank Stapleton to supply the assured finishing touch. 'It bounced perfectly for me,' recalled the goalscorer. 'It would have been the miss of all time but I didn't have time to think about it and just volleyed it home.'

## WHAT THE PAPERS SAID

'This wasn't an occasion for applying the jargon-laden criteria fed to hearth-rug audiences. It was a touch of the old-time religion, the tribal fervour that reminds us of how deeply football can still affect a huge mass of working-class people in this country. The atmosphere at Old Trafford in midweek was like a hot, feverish wind from another time.'

Hugh McIlvanney, *The Times*

This was exciting, attacking football in the best traditions of the club. 'It was the type of night when you had goose-bumps on your neck and your arms,' said Whiteside. 'Players and fans alike. You could really feel the atmosphere.'

An away goal would still have taken Cesar Luis Menotti's team through, depriving United of a first European semi-final for 15 years. Substitute Mark Hughes was perhaps fortunate not to concede a penalty, Schuster shot wide, Bailey kept out Julio Alberto and Maradona fired a free-kick into the side-netting.

'The problem was we took the third goal too early,' said Atkinson afterwards, his nerves clearly frayed. 'It's a pity we couldn't have got it in the eighty-sixth minute. But that's what European football is really about.'

When Italian referee Paolo Casarin brought an end to proceedings, with Kevin Moran rushing down the pitch with the ball oblivious to the final whistle, there was unbridled joy and a sense that one of the greatest performances since Sir Matt Busby's reign had been witnessed.

The great man himself drew comparisons with his classic team of the 1950s and was clearly proud to see his traditions being upheld. 'The memories came flooding back,' he stated. 'The game took me right back to the time we pulled back two goals against Bilbao at Maine Road for that memorable win in our first season in Europe.'

Robson was feted by fans at the end who chanted his name in a bid to ram home the message that the Serie A suitors needed to be fended off. 'A lot of fans invaded the pitch and carried me off on their shoulders,' he added. 'I remember I was a long way from the tunnel at the whistle, so there was no chance to get inside before the crowd mobbed me. That night was the best atmosphere I experienced during my thirteen years as a player here. You could feel the pitch shaking that night.'

Robson's midfield partner, Wilkins, did end up moving to Italy with AC Milan, while Juventus were mercifully unable to meet United's £3 million asking price for the England captain. Wilkins felt the duo never played better in all their matches together for club and country. 'After the game, I never slept a wink,' he admitted. 'For days, I was on an adrenalin rush.'

Every supporter felt the same insomnia after a glorious occasion that will live forever in the memory. Juventus lost the battle for Robson but would emerge victorious in the semi-finals against an injury-ravaged United line-up, yet nothing could ever detract from the most glorious of comebacks against the cream of the continent; the night when the decibel bar was set for all future nights under the floodlights.

## THE TEAMS

**Manchester United:** Bailey; Duxbury, Moran, Hogg, Albiston; Muhren, Wilkins, Robson, Moses; Stapleton, Whiteside (Hughes 72)

**Subs not used:** Pears, Graham, Gidman, McGrath

**Goalscorers:** Robson 23, 51, Stapleton 53

**Barcelona:** Urruti; Gerardo, Julio Alberto, Alesanco, Moratalla; Alonso (Clos 57), Victor, Schuster, Rojo; Maradona, Marcos

**Subs not used:** Olmo, Artoia, Manola, Esteban

# 5 MANCHESTER UNITED 4
## SL BENFICA 1

**European Cup final**
**29 May 1968**
**Wembley Stadium, London**

## THE HOLY GRAIL

If ever a football match transcended the sport, perhaps it was this one. A decade after Matt Busby's dreams of conquering the continent lay shattered in the wreckage at Munich-Riem Airport, the great man realised his personal nirvana on a hot and humid night at Wembley.

'When Bobby [Charlton] took the cup, it cleansed me,' said the manager who rebuilt a team good enough to lift the trophy he and his Babes had coveted so fiercely. 'It eased the pain of the guilt of going into Europe. It was my justification.'

The nation was fully behind the blues of Manchester United, something unthinkable in today's partisan times, as a remarkable goal-burst in the first half of extra time ensured an English name was finally written on the trophy. Even without Denis Law – hospitalised by knee surgery – United had enough firepower to overpower Benfica and, fittingly, Charlton, one of the survivors of the crash, scored two of the goals.

'This is the most wonderful thing that has happened in my life,' sighed Busby afterwards. 'I have had a lot of disappointments, but this has made up for everything. At the moment, I'm the proudest man in England.'

Shay Brennan revealed that Paddy Crerand told the players to 'win it for Matt' in the dressing room beforehand. 'That's what it was all about,' said the full-back. 'He had the vision to push the club into Europe in 1956 when the Football League was dead against it. This was his testimonial.'

The final blockade facing Busby and his side was Benfica. Though a mighty presence spearheaded by the legendary Eusebio, the Reds' Lisbon rout against the Portuguese champions two years earlier had claimed the psychological high ground for United. There was nothing to fear.

Once the game began, it followed a predictable path. 'Finals tend to be boring and the first half was boring,' admitted goalkeeper Alex Stepney. An extra frisson of excitement accompanied every touch by George Best, however, even if the winger came in for some rough treatment from his markers and occasionally let his temper flare. On the other flank, there was positive flair from John Aston, who knew he had the beating of Adolfo Calisto for pace and proceeded to prove it time and time again with breathtaking acceleration.

'I'm not being immodest but, if they'd had a man of the match award, I think I would have won it,' said Aston, with plenty of justification. 'I had grown up idolising Bill Foulkes, Charlton and Brennan, and to play alongside them in their first European Cup final was very special for me.'

David Sadler could not convert a Paddy Crerand free-kick at full stretch, while Eusebio came closest to breaking the deadlock in the first half when a right-footed drive cannoned against the bar following a forceful run. 'I never even saw it,' admitted Stepney. Brian Kidd, on his 19th birthday, had an effort blocked and also did superbly to tee up Sadler, only for the forward to spurn the opportunity with a wasteful finish.

Sadler was to atone for his miss eight minutes after the interval when he floated over a cross from the left that Charlton met with a precise glancing nod past Henrique. 'I didn't know my header had gone in for the first goal,' said the scorer. 'This must be the first time I've headed a goal in about ten years.'

When Best mesmerised the defence, leaving three men trailing in his wake, it should have led to a second goal, but Henrique not only thwarted the Northern Irishman but also Sadler from the rebound with his legs.

However, Benfica grew in stature and started to apply more pressure of their own, Eusebio lashing over a promising opening. With 15 minutes remaining, Torres headed down a Jose Augusto cross and, although the ball skipped past Eusebio, Jaime Graca was on hand to show great technique in volleying past Stepney.

Eusebio really should have won it for the Portuguese champions, but shot at Stepney after an exhilarating run and then could only fire the ball into the keeper's midriff after being released by Antonio Simoes's delightful pass on the break. 'I was not in good shape,' the Portugal striker recalled. 'They found a small fracture later in my right knee. So I moved the ball to my left. It was a good shot but straight into Stepney's chest. If it had been my other foot, Benfica would have won that European Cup.'

After sportingly applauding the keeper's stop, the 'Black Pearl' then planted a header the wrong side of the post as extra time was required for the first time in a European Cup final. 'We were all shattered but so were Benfica,' said Nobby Stiles. 'When we looked around, they were in a worse plight than us. Once we all sensed this, we really began to play.'

Benfica had ended normal time in the ascendancy, but their defence was all at sea when failing to deal with Stepney's long punt three minutes after the restart. Kidd headed on and

Best pounced to dance his way through and around Henrique to claim a wonderful solo strike, contrary to the famous TV commentary that he 'simply walked the ball home'.

Indeed, Best said much later: 'I always find it frustrating when my goal is shown on TV because you only see me taking the ball around the keeper. I'd stuck it through the centre-half's legs and was more chuffed with that than anything. I thought about walking it in, or stopping it on the line and kneeling down to head it in, but finally thought better of it.'

From the next attack, Aston sped down the left like an express train again to win a corner and, when Charlton's flag-kick was headed back by Sadler, Kidd was on hand to score at the second attempt with a looping header after Henrique halted his initial effort. 'Fortunately it rebounded at just the right height and pace and I nodded it back over him,' remembered Kidd.

Teenager Kidd then combined well with Charlton and delivered a perfect return pass for the World Cup winner to clip a delightful finish into the net for his second goal and United's fourth. There was still plenty of time left, but there was no way back for Benfica, even if Eusebio forced another save from Stepney.

There were emotional scenes at the end and Charlton was in tears as he embraced Busby. 'When they equalised, I felt so bad I didn't think I'd ever pull myself together again,' he said. 'But, although they had exceptional ability, we were stronger and better prepared. We outlasted Real Madrid in the semis, which was the real final, and then we outlasted Benfica.'

The players failed in a bid to persuade the manager to break with tradition and collect the trophy himself. 'We did it for Sir Matt,' stressed Charlton. 'We wanted to win for the boss.' Yet there was the feeling this was mission accomplished and an end of a golden era.

So it proved, with United going into the comparative doldrums until the return of sustained success in the 1990s. Foulkes, like Charlton a survivor of Munich, was less romantic than others about the joy at the end of a long personal quest. 'We had to win it,' he asserted. 'Maybe there was a touch of destiny about it all. At the end, I was accused of

being unemotional, but I'd been through hell since Munich and I had done my emoting after the semi-final in Madrid.'

Tony Dunne perhaps summed it up best. 'Afterwards was a terrible anti-climax,' he insisted. 'When you have been trying to win something so much for someone – a team had died trying to do it – then when you actually achieve it, there was only relief.'

Relief had replaced grief as the overriding emotion on a night when the contest itself seemed almost secondary. For United and Busby, the long journey to the peak of European football was finally over.

## THE TEAMS

**Manchester United:** Stepney; Brennan, Dunne; Foulkes, Crerand, Stiles; Best, Kidd, Charlton, Sadler, Aston

**Sub not used:** Rimmer

**Goalscorers:** Charlton 53, 99, Best 93, Kidd 94

**SL Benfica:** Henrique; Adolfo, Humberto, Jacinto, Cruz; Graca, Coluna, Jose Augusto; Torres, Eusebio, Simoes

**Sub not used:** Nascimento

**Goalscorer:** Graca 75

# 4

## JUVENTUS 2
## MANCHESTER UNITED 3

**Champions League semi-final, second leg**
**21 April 1999**
**Stadio delle Alpi, Turin**

# FULL SPEED AHEAD, BARCELONA

If few gave United a chance of progressing to the Champions League final before kick-off at the Stadio delle Alpi, fewer still would have offered them a prayer after Filippo Inzaghi's two goals inside the opening 11 minutes embossed the Italians' existing away-goal advantage.

Before dissecting one of the greatest of all the Reds' miraculous comebacks, its proper context must first be digested. Juventus were playing in a record 55th consecutive European Cup game, bidding to reach a fourth successive final and fielding a veritable European dream team containing the reigning World Footballer of the Year Zinedine Zidane. Despite some rich pedigree in the competition, United had never even won on Italian soil and the club's only appearance in the final came 31 years previously.

'As far as most are concerned, United are already out, Juventus are as good as in the final and tonight's match will hold all the surprise value of rain on a Bank Holiday,' wrote the *Daily Mail*'s Graham Hunter on the morning of battle. 'There is a small pocket of red resistance emanating from England, but that is about it.'

Yet Ryan Giggs's late equaliser at Old Trafford had not only breathed life into Alex Ferguson's bid to reach his first final at this level, it had also exposed signs of weariness in the black-and-white ranks in the first leg. 'We have good stamina,' Jaap Stam prophetically warned before the sides reconvened in Turin.

Giggs was an absentee through injury, however, and an uncomfortable situation became decidedly more painful following the early skirmishes, even if Andy Cole did thud an overhead kick into Angelo Peruzzi's midriff. Inzaghi met a Zidane cross ahead of Gary Neville to smuggle in the opener, then claimed a fortuitous second when he spun away from Stam, shot against the underside of the Dutchman's leg and watched Peter Schmeichel wave the ball on its way with a despairing swipe of his giant right hand as it looped into the net.

Top Italian sides, always notoriously difficult to break down, simply did not fail from such a position of strength on their home territory. Except, there is a first time for everything – a point illustrated by Roy Keane's determination to burst into the box to glance home David Beckham's corner. It was the first headed goal of his lengthy United career.

Although it highlighted his sheer professionalism to march back to the halfway line with no fanfare, a greater indicator of his temperament was to follow. Jesper Blomqvist, Giggs's stand-in, was guilty of a poor pass, which Keane miscontrolled. In trying to retrieve the situation, the Irishman fouled Zidane and received a booking that would trigger a suspension. 'I remember his eyes when he looked at me after that tackle,' recounted Blomqvist. '"It's your fault that I'm going to miss the final."' Despite his personal tragedy, Keane refocused and produced a performance many reckon to be his best ever for the club.

'He seemed to redouble his efforts,' praised Ferguson. 'He showed that concern for others which separates truly special people. I didn't think Roy could go up any further in my estimation than he was, but he did in that game.'

After surviving a real scare when the outstanding Stam headed off the line with Schmeichel stranded, strike duo Cole and Dwight Yorke worked their near-telepathic magic. Beckham headed a long ball by Gary Neville back to Cole and his lofted cross was propelled past Peruzzi by a diving Yorke. United suddenly led on away goals. 'Once Yorkie got the second goal, I was pretty sure this was going to be our night,' confessed Schmeichel.

## WHAT THE PAPERS SAID

On a night of unrelenting, escalating and scarcely credible football drama at a packed, intense, evocative stadium at the foothills of the Alps, Manchester United conquered the highest summit yet in Alex Ferguson's triumphant 13 years at Old Trafford. Last night, United planted a glorious red flag on one of Europe's most prestigious peaks and it is their vivid colours that will fly high over Camp Nou in Barcelona next month.

Michael Walker, *Guardian*

The front pairing combined again for Yorke to crash a drive against the woodwork with Ferguson exclaiming: 'The first forty-five minutes were among the best I've ever seen United play in all the years I've been in charge.'

Carlo Ancelotti threw on an extra striker, Nicola Amoruso, at the interval in retaliation, but it was Inzaghi who continued to carry most of the threat, having his hat-trick celebrations cut short only by a linesman's flag. 'That lad was born offside,' the manager once famously said of the Italy international.

Back came United, with Denis Irwin encouraged to continue a run forward and lash a fine effort against a post with Peruzzi beaten, before drilling the rebound into the Italian's side-netting. Paul Scholes then joined Keane in collecting a costly booking that would rule him out of the final. 'Dider Deschamps jumped in with both feet and I was just trying to protect myself,' explained the substitute. 'When the referee blew, I thought it would have been a free-kick to us.'

The Reds may have been ahead by the narrowest of margins, but another strike was surely going to be required and it arrived when Paolo Montero made a mess of Schmeichel's booming kick. Yorke pounced and burst enterprisingly between the Uruguayan and Ciro Ferrara, nimbly staying on his feet until Peruzzi took them from him. With everybody screaming for a penalty, and a red card, time stood still as Cole alertly ran onto the loose ball and, from an ever-decreasing angle, slipped the ball inside the near post. 'Full speed ahead, Barcelona,' ITV commentator Clive Tyldesley famously crowed.

Nicky Butt declared afterwards: 'I think we finally proved to ourselves that we have come of age. We're men now, not young boys still learning.' Yet this was a triumph, not only for a youthful side that had earned its stripes in continental combat, but also for the manager. 'We met a team that was tactically superior to us,' conceded Ancelotti. 'We couldn't control the game in midfield and were forced to play long balls, but we couldn't get past their two strong defenders in front of the box.'

Stam, in particular, pushed up to shackle Zidane, who had been identified as the key man beforehand. 'We were willing to risk one against one at the back to apply the methods we knew could win us the match,' explained Ferguson. 'The way we played showed we can cope with tactical changes in a game of that importance. Tactically, we were very good.'

While Keane rampaged around midfield, Cole was outstanding in stretching the defence by moving wide and Yorke dropped deep to exert more influence and confuse the Bianconeri defenders. 'We played it into the channels and Cole and Yorke were causing them nightmares,' recalled Gary Neville.

An evening that had started with orchestrated chanting from the Ultras on the Curva Nord ended with even the partisan home fans acknowledging their conquerors' achievement. 'We heard the Juventus supporters applauding us at the end and that shows they appreciated the way we never gave up,' said Stam. 'We showed them we could play and I think it inspired them into a great gesture.'

Stam must have had a premonition of the unprecedented glory that would follow in the coming weeks. 'Nothing is beyond us,' roared the indomitable Netherlander. 'We are a great team and everyone is desperate to win these prizes. I have never played in a team with so much belief.' After an unbelievable comeback in Turin, even greater drama was to follow in the final.

## THE TEAMS

**Juventus:** Peruzzi; Birindelli (Amoruso 46), Ferrara, Iuliano (Montero 46), Pessotto; Conte, Deschamps, Davids, Di Livio (Fonseca 80); Zidane; Inzaghi

**Subs not used:** Rampulla, Tudor

**Goalscorer:** Inzaghi 6, 11

**Manchester United:** Schmeichel; G.Neville, Stam, Johnsen, Irwin; Beckham, Butt, Keane, Blomqvist (Scholes 68); Yorke, Cole

**Subs not used:** van der Gouw, May, Sheringham, P.Neville

**Goalscorers:** Keane 24, Yorke 34, Cole 83

# 3 MANCHESTER UNITED 2 ARSENAL 1

**FA Cup semi-final replay**
**14 April 1999**
**Villa Park, Birmingham**

## WINNER TAKES ALL

United and Arsenal. The two top teams in England, fierce rivals on the field and in the dugouts, in a late-season FA Cup fight to the finish with ramifications on an equally absorbing title race; even the most rudimentary synopsis screams 'blockbuster.'

What unfolded lived up to the billing. Spectacular goals, pitch invasions, a disallowed goal, a red card and an injury-time penalty stop which saved a season; no amount of words could ever convey the emotive nature of a genuine classic in which United's Treble bid straddled a knife-edge before plunging a dagger into Arsenal's hearts.

As a spectacle, it may never be matched for quality, incident and drama. Subplot after absorbing subplot contrived and interwove to fashion the perfect football spectacle, won in extra time through a goal by Ryan Giggs that stands comparison with any scored in United's history.

And to think: the game shouldn't even have taken place.

Three days earlier, the sides met in another engaging Villa Park tussle that was most notable for an extraordinary decision by referee David Elleray to disallow Roy Keane's first-half goal for offside. The Irishman slammed home after Dwight Yorke had headed on Giggs's cross, only for the goal to be chalked off because Yorke was ahead of play when Giggs nudged the ball forward to himself. Though United were incensed, Elleray retorted: 'I slept reasonably well on Sunday night.'

'It was absolutely ridiculous,' scoffed Alex Ferguson. 'I have watched it on TV and it's quite amazing. But it doesn't matter. It wasn't a goal and we have just got to get on with it.' With another taxing fixture crowbarred into an already daunting calendar, the manager made four personnel changes for the replay, as Giggs, Yorke, Andy Cole and Denis Irwin made way for Jesper Blomqvist, Teddy Sheringham, Ole Gunnar Solskjaer and Phil Neville. Arsène Wenger, meanwhile, welcomed back

Emmanuel Petit after suspension and fielded him at the expense of Nelson Vivas, while the jaded Marc Overmars was benched in favour of Freddie Ljungberg.

While the Gunners were strengthened by the restoration of Petit's famed central midfield partnership with Patrick Vieira, it was United who began brighter and struck the first goal of the game. Hitherto, Arsenal hadn't conceded a goal in 11½ hours of football; breaching their fabled defence required something special.

As Vieira's half-hit volley bobbled through to him, Peter Schmeichel had already spotted Solskjaer attempting to find space behind Martin Keown. The Dane's hefty punt only found the Arsenal defender, but his poor header fell to the onrushing David Beckham, who struggled to bridle the ball but eventually nudged it to Sheringham. The striker considered his options, allowed space to develop and teed up Beckham to whip a wonderful 25-yard effort into David Seaman's bottom corner.

United's breakneck start continued as Sheringham shot wide, then headed a yard past the upright, before Ray Parlour posed Arsenal's first question of Schmeichel with a fizzing drive. The Gunners emerged as an attacking force only as half time approached, and they carried the momentum into the second period – even though the restart was delayed as Petit sought a pair of mittens to guard against the chill of the English spring.

Penned back but comfortable, United increasingly looked to counter-attack. When Tony Adams failed to cut out Ronny Johnsen's clearing header, Solskjaer strode through on goal and, despite the attentions of Keown, rifled in a shot which Seaman brilliantly clutched on his goal line.

**MANCHESTER UNITED 2 – ARSENAL 1**

The tie might have been settled then. Instead, it was nudged back into the balance on 69 minutes as Nigel Winterburn's pass infield found Dennis Bergkamp. The Dutchman dropped between Johnsen and Keane, turned and took on an early, long-range shot that struck Jaap Stam on the knee and bounced beyond the helpless Schmeichel.

'That Arsenal team between 1997 and 1999 was the best domestic team I ever faced,' confirmed Gary Neville, and United were suddenly weathering an almighty storm from the reigning Premier League champions. Though the Reds' defiance wavered, it was never extinguished in a torrid final 20 minutes.

Substitute Nicolas Anelka tucked in a close-range finish after Bergkamp's shot had been parried by Schmeichel, only for a linesman's flag to correctly chalk it off. Unaware, Arsenal's players and pitch-invading supporters celebrated for over 30 seconds before realising what had happened. Their ignorance provoked much mirth from the 20,000 or so United fans, whose relief was instantly dashed as Keane lunged into a challenge on substitute Overmars, prompting a second yellow card and mandatory red accompaniment for the United skipper.

Though there was plentiful late pressure, Arsenal forged no openings until injury time, when Parlour's run into the area was clumsily halted by Phil Neville, prompting the incontestable award of a penalty. It was make or break for United except, curiously, in the mind of the man on whom their hopes rested. 'I didn't know it was the last minute,' laughs Schmeichel. 'I thought that if Arsenal scored we still had ten minutes to try and equalise!'

Regardless of his blissful ignorance, the giant Dane sprung to United's rescue by spectacularly parrying away Bergkamp's spot-kick and injecting life back into the Treble dream. Schmeichel prolonged it in the first period of extra time with a stunning full-length stop to keep out Bergkamp's rasper from just inside the box. As an attacking force, United were spent, like a punch-drunk boxer clinging to the ropes and hoping to hear the bell.

Then, from nothing, came everything. Vieira played a wearied pass in search of Lee Dixon, but instead found a bare, yawning lawn ten yards inside the Arsenal half. 'From nowhere, as if he's just popped up out of the ground, Ryan got on the ball,' recounts the United manager. 'Steve McClaren, myself and Jim Ryan are going: "Take it in the corner flag," because by that time we were down to ten men and getting to penalties gave us a chance. "Take it in the corner flag ... go on, run it to the corner flag."'

The Arsenal defence, though suddenly called on alert, were unperturbed. 'I remember thinking:

"It's okay because he's in front of me and I've got plenty of time to get back,"' recalls Dixon. 'I turned and saw we had our back four more or less in position. A bit of a breakaway, but no real danger.'

It took Giggs just 11 touches to move the ball 55 yards, bypassing challenges from Vieira, Dixon, Keown and Dixon again before Adams hurtled across to try to make a last-ditch block. 'I think he was tired by then because he beat us so many times he thought "I'll just lash it,"' smiles Dixon.

The left-footed shot, from deep within the Arsenal area but at a daunting angle, was like a detonation in terms of power and devastation. As it crossed the line, Seaman, Adams and Keown were strewn prostrate about the turf, looking upwards to see it thunder into the roof of the net. Bedlam ensued, along with a celebration just as memorable as the goal itself.

Giggs, now running along the touchline at full pelt, whipped off his shirt and whirled it around his head, exposing a rarely seen hirsute chest to an unsuspecting audience – a small price for both parties to pay. About him, fans spilled onto the field and were sucked into his slipstream, along with his incredulous team-mates. By the time the celebratory huddle had settled on the touchline, Giggs had around 40 well-wishers extolling their gratitude.

'I've never done a celebration like that before,' he grins. 'To be honest with you it was a bit of a relief because I'd come on as sub and I'd given the ball away three or four times, so I was having a bit of a beast and obviously that got me out of it. I don't know what I was thinking. I don't know why I did it. Like the goal, it was purely instinctive, and I just thought: "Who cares?" If I could go back I'd probably change it. Never mind.'

The dribs and drabs of supporters who had trickled onto the field to join Giggs in celebration were among a flood of fans who poured on as the final whistle sounded. United's exhausted players had nowhere to go, nor the energy to take them there. Some were chaired from the field shoulder-high by jubilant supporters, in scenes worthy of some overblown Hollywood climax but somehow entirely apt for the preceding events.

The thrilling victory may not have had the last-gasp plot twist of the tale that would unfold in Camp Nou, but for the sheer, blinding entertainment served up by a galaxy of stars at Villa Park, it lays serious claim to being the most absorbing epic in United's history.

## THE TEAMS

**Arsenal:** Seaman; Dixon, Keown, Adams, Winterburn; Parlour (Kanu 105), Vieira, Petit (Bould 119), Ljungberg (Overmars 62); Bergkamp, Anelka

**Subs not used:** Lukic, Vivas

**Goalscorer:** Bergkamp 69

**Manchester United:** Schmeichel; G.Neville, Johnsen, Stam, P.Neville; Beckham, Keane, Butt, Blomqvist (Giggs 62); Sheringham (Scholes 76), Solskjaer (Yorke 91)

**Subs not used:** van der Gouw, Irwin

**Goalscorers:** Beckham 17, Giggs 109

# 2 MANCHESTER UNITED 1
# CHELSEA 1

**(United win 6-5 on penalties)**
**Champions League final**
**22 May 2008**
**Luzhniki Stadium, Moscow**

## THE HISTORY BOYS

Some things are just meant to be. Fifty years on from Munich and 40 years after Matt Busby had led United to their first continental triumph, fate contrived to crown the Reds champions of Europe for a third time after a nerve-shredding game of Russian roulette in Moscow.

United bested Chelsea after 120 minutes of football and a penalty shoot-out that oscillated wildly between the two teams in the first all-English Champions League final. The Reds took a long, hard look down the barrel of defeat – benefiting from rainfall of near-biblical proportions which caused John Terry to slip and miss his kick – before snatching victory when Edwin van der Sar saved from Nicolas Anelka.

United had looked set to pay the price for Cristiano Ronaldo's failure to score from the spot, despite the Portuguese capping a quite ludicrous season's work with the opening goal

in normal time. He and his colleagues – along with the worldwide Red Army, peeping through parted fingers – were ultimately spared, however, in fateful circumstances. 'Fate does play its part,' beamed Sir Alex Ferguson. 'I'm a firm believer in that. You wouldn't think such a thing was possible.'

The Reds' third European rule was a fitting honour for the side, he later admitted, 'could well be' the best he had ever helmed. There was the power and speed of the 1993-94 Double winners, the bloody-minded invincibility of the Treble winners, and then there was the swagger and verve of the 2007-08 vintage, who sliced through all-comers at home and abroad. In Chelsea, they met foes who pushed them all the way on both platforms.

United had landed the first blow ten days before the final, retaining their Premier League title on the final day of the season and seeing off a late surge from Avram Grant's side. The Israeli had commendably hauled the Blues into domestic contention and through the Champions League, despite replacing Jose Mourinho in only a temporary capacity. Now they faced a United side standing on the brink of special elevation. 'You're only really considered a great player at this club when you win the Champions League,' Rio Ferdinand opined.

The mechanical power of Chelsea compared to the free-flowing incision of United presented an intriguing clash of styles for both managers to ponder, and Sir Alex sprang a huge surprise in deploying Cristiano Ronaldo on the left wing in the hope that Blues midfielder Michael Essien would moonlight at right-back. Sure enough, the Ghanaian lined up in defence.

Owen Hargreaves filled Ronaldo's usual berth on the right flank, while Paul Scholes and Michael Carrick anchored central midfield. The duo would be outnumbered by Claude Makelele, Frank Lampard and Michael Ballack in the Blues' 4-3-3 set-up, but great rewards prompt great risks.

After a cagey opening to the game, in which Scholes broke his nose in an accidental-but-ugly clash with Makelele, Sir Alex's gamble paid off. Neat interplay between Scholes and Wes Brown on the right flank gave Brown time to pick out a cross for Ronaldo. Essien's unfamiliarity

with his duties shone through as he failed to get tight to his man and watched on as the Portuguese winger soared high, directed his header past the motionless Petr Cech and bagged his 42nd goal of a staggering season.

Chelsea, who had offered little in attack, almost drew level on 34 minutes when Ballack's presence – and shove – forced Ferdinand into heading towards his own goal. Despite the point-blank range of the header, van der Sar was alert enough to beat it away to safety.

United broke forward from the resulting corner, and Wayne Rooney found Ronaldo with an exquisite 60-yard cross-field pass. The winger controlled it brilliantly and delivered a perfect cross onto Carlos Tevez's head. Cech blocked the diving effort from the Argentine and was also on hand to brilliantly fend away Carrick's follow-up shot from the edge of the box.

Two minutes before the break, Hargreaves won possession, broke forward and fed Rooney on the right. The striker fizzed in an early cross that evaded Makelele at the front post and the stretching Tevez just behind him. United should have been home and hosed when the interval came. Instead, they were merely level.

After Essien's shot cannoned off both Nemanja Vidic and Ferdinand, it dropped to Lampard in the area. Van der Sar raced to meet him but slipped at the vital moment, allowing the

Chelsea midfielder to side-foot home. Somehow the scores were level, and the goal had contrasting effects on both sides.

United were sapped of momentum and confidence, while Chelsea played with renewed vim and vigour. The Londoners were unable to find a route past the Vidic–Ferdinand axis, however, though they and all of a Red persuasion watched on in horror 12 minutes from time when Didier Drogba arced a right-foot shot against van der Sar's left-hand post with the Dutchman well beaten.

Lampard repeated the trick four minutes into extra time when he spun to thud a shot against the underside of the United crossbar. By that point, Ryan Giggs had entered the fray, breaking Sir Bobby Charlton's all-time appearance record in his 759th match for the Reds, and the veteran winger almost capped his record-breaking night with a winning goal. Patrice Evra brilliantly burst into the area before pulling the ball back, and Giggs's toe-poked effort was goalbound until Terry somehow contorted to head the ball over the bar.

United were reinvigorated, but the game descended into minor farce in the second period of extra time. Chelsea's players reacted angrily to perceived poor sportsmanship, after Tevez had kicked the ball out for a throw-in rather than return it to the Blues after a stoppage (even though Salomon Kalou had done exactly the same thing in the first period of extra time) and, in the resultant scuffle, Drogba needlessly aimed a slap at Vidic and was sent off.

## WHAT THE PAPERS SAID

'After this incredible victory in the biggest game in the history of British club football, there can be no quibbling about what Sir Alex Ferguson has achieved. Now he has kept his promise to the men of Munich that he would not let them down 50 years after the air disaster that claimed the lives of so many of the Busby Babes. That sentiment and the fact that Ferguson has always produced teams that thrill the soul made it feel as though United's victory in this enthralling match was a victory for the spirit of the game.

'A victory for a club that has stayed loyal to a manager. And a manager that has stayed loyal to a club. A victory for football's last dictator and for the principle that a manager decides. A victory for playing football the right way. For trying to win a match. Rather than trying not to lose one. But however lavish the tributes to Ferguson this morning, the most sumptuous tribute of all was the one provided by his players during the match. Some of the football they played on an occasion which often stifles creativity and expression was breathtakingly beautiful.'

Oliver Holt, *Daily Mirror*

With Drogba ruled out of the ensuing shoot-out, a hasty rejig followed on both sides. Sir Alex needed to essentially dismiss one of his players to level the sides at ten players apiece, and it was decided that Evra would not take a penalty. A Blue-clad defender, however, was putting his hand up for duties.

'Terry was not on the list,' revealed Grant, 'but because Drogba was out, we changed it because Kalou needed to be the fifth and then, because it was the deciding penalty, JT wanted it.'

Nine other players would step up before Terry, however, starting with Tevez, who slotted home without fuss. Ballack followed suit. Then up came the first Englishman in the shoot-out: Carrick. 'I just said to myself: "Please score,"' he recalled. 'You know there's always going to be someone who's going to have to miss and you pray it's not you.'

It wouldn't be substitute Juliano Belletti either. However, forward stepped Ronaldo, hero of United's

season, only to see his shot blocked by Cech's face. 'I thought it would be the worst day of my life,' admitted an ashen-faced Ronaldo.

Now the pressure was on van der Sar to rescue his side. He mustered a touch to Lampard's effort, but was unable to prevent Chelsea moving into the lead for the first time. Next up, Hargreaves. 'I thought everybody knew which way I was going to go,' recalled the midfielder. 'I thought: "I'm going to have to change spots", I was going to put it in the other corner. But when I got there and looked at the goal I thought: "Jeez that looks small!" So I just put it where I normally would.' Top corner. 3-3.

Hargreaves's England colleague, Ashley Cole, was Chelsea's next taker. Van der Sar reached his effort but could only paw it into his own side netting. Ditto Cech's attempts to save from Nani with United's fifth kick. Then came Mr Chelsea, adjusting his captain's armband as he approached. Terry exuded confidence in his stance and run-up, but slipped at the key moment and sent his effort against the outside of van der Sar's post. Behind the Dutchman's goal, 25,000 United fans leapt and writhed in delight. Game on.

Substitutes Anderson and Giggs both converted kicks of contrasting precision – the former thumped down the centre, the latter whipped into the corner – which bookended Kalou's nonchalant conversion for Chelsea. 'I fancied saving the one from Kalou, but it didn't happen,' recounted van der Sar. 'Luckily, I got one right!'

And how. The Dutchman flung himself to his right and landed into club legend by parrying away Anelka's effort, simultaneously uncorking a stampede of team-mates and colleagues. 'You see it coming, you save it and then you get up and you know the game's over,' grinned the Dutchman. 'You have two, three or four seconds on your own, arms in the air and everything goes through your mind. You see your team-mates coming towards you and it's just happiness; one of the greatest feelings you can ever have.'

Amid all the shared joy which ensued, however, came a poignant reminder of United's opulent history as club director Sir Bobby Charlton, a survivor of 1958 and a two-goal hero at Wembley ten years later, was awarded a winner's medal by UEFA. At the squad's post-match party, the club's all-time leading goalscorer, having just surrendered his longstanding appearances record, presented his successor, Giggs, with a watch simply inscribed '759'.

'We thought about Munich and 1968 before the game,' admitted Carrick. 'When the match started we were focused on that, but when we'd actually won and we saw Sir Bobby on the pitch and going up with us for the cup, it was very emotional for everyone. That's when the achievement really sunk in.'

For Carrick and his colleagues, their prize extended beyond the sweat-soaked glory of lifting the biggest prize in club football; they had added another glorious chapter to United's epic history.

## THE TEAMS

**Manchester United:** van der Sar; Brown (Anderson 120), Ferdinand, Vidic, Evra; Hargreaves, Carrick, Scholes (Giggs 88); Ronaldo; Tevez, Rooney (Nani 101)

**Subs not used:** Kuszczak, O'Shea, Fletcher, Silvestre

**Goalscorer:** Ronaldo 26

**Chelsea:** Cech; Essien, Carvalho, Terry, A.Cole; Makelele (Belletti 120); J.Cole (Anelka 98), Lampard, Ballack, Malouda (Kalou 92); Drogba

**Subs not used:** Cudicini, Shevchenko, Mikel, Alex

**Goalscorer:** Lampard 45

# 1

## MANCHESTER UNITED 2
## BAYERN MUNICH 1

**Champions League final**
**26 May 1999**
**Camp Nou, Barcelona**

# FOOTBALL, BLOODY HELL

And Solskjaer has won it. Surprised? Could any other game really have put forward a stronger case than that which elevated United to a zenith of glory and emotion beyond reality's boundaries?

Winning the Champions League is a momentous achievement. Doing so within 11 days of insatiably sweeping up the Premier League title and FA Cup elevates it beyond staggering. Hauling it back from the jaws of defeat and securing it with two goals in three injury-time minutes engraves United's 1999 triumph just a little deeper than the rest in club football's grandest trophy.

'Football, bloody hell,' Alex Ferguson famously remarked after the final whistle. Even he, who knew his side better than anybody, didn't foresee that they could wring themselves of two final drops of inspiration at the end of a season characterised by character.

One of the finest Arsenal teams of all time was vanquished in an absorbing Premier League title race. The Gunners, along with title challengers Chelsea and perennial rivals Liverpool were deposed en route to an FA Cup success which brought the club's third domestic Double. It was in Europe, however, where the sternest questions were posed.

In danger of being cast as nearly men after heartbreaking near-misses in 1996-97 and 1997-98, a group draw that pitted the Reds against Bayern, Barcelona and Brondby suggested that 1998-99 would be their biggest test yet. When they emerged unscathed from that taxing quartet, fate threw up bookies' favourites Internazionale and then a Juventus side shooting for a fourth straight final. Having clawed their way over those sizable hurdles, United were faced once more with Ottmar Hitzfeld's Bayern.

Not that the clubs' group stage

meetings gave cause for trepidation. Only a last-minute rush of blood from Peter Schmeichel had given the Germans a 2-2 draw in the Olympiastadion, while a 1-1 stalemate at Old Trafford suited both sides and passed without either committing to attack.

There was, however, cause for concern in midfield, where United's heart had been wrenched away. Both Roy Keane and Paul Scholes would sit out the final through suspension, prompting the repurposing of David Beckham as a central midfielder alongside Nicky Butt, with Jesper Blomqvist on the left flank and Ryan Giggs on the right. Originally, the Welshman had been pencilled in for a central berth in order to expose the lack of pace of Lothar Matthaus, but Beckham's impressive cameo in the FA Cup final victory over Newcastle prompted a rethink from the United management.

One of three team-talks the day before the final focused on how the German side had overcome Dynamo Kiev in their semi-final. Level on aggregate but cushioned by away goals after a 3-3 first-leg draw, Hitzfeld's side had forged ahead through Mario Basler's strike before putting down the shutters and seeing out a comfortable progress to the final.

Irritation swept through the United ranks, then, when Basler fired the Bundesliga champions ahead at Camp Nou after only six minutes.

The German international rifled a low shot around Schmeichel's wall, into space vacated by decoy brick Markus Babbel, and the ball hurtled past the motionless Dane.

'Once ahead, Bayern made it difficult for us, as expected,' rued Ferguson. Hitzfeld's troops retreated, with Stefan Effenberg and Jens Jeremies predictably dominant in central midfield against the unfamiliar Beckham–Butt axis, while the former's absence from the right flank meant the supply line to Andy Cole and Dwight Yorke was less fruitful than usual.

Nevertheless, United's play slowly grew in confidence as the first period wore on. 'After conceding, we started to fall into our normal rhythm,' recalled Schmeichel. 'We started to calm down and we knew what we had to do now: we had to score. Having that knowledge that we must score made us a very dangerous team to play against. Their mentality was to cling on to what they had. I was pretty sure that at some point we would score and 1-1 would give us momentum. I didn't have the feeling that we were going to wait as long as we did!'

The game meandered through the first half without a further opportunity of note. United's attacking intent shone through, but couldn't pierce a Bayern side defending tigerishly. Ten minutes after the break, however, a chink in the Germans' armour appeared. Giggs whipped in a cross from the right and Blomqvist stole behind Babbel to reach the ball on the half-volley, but the Swede could only jab his finish high over Oliver Kahn's crossbar.

Blomqvist was sacrificed on 66 minutes as Alex Ferguson sought to alter his side's approach. On went Teddy Sheringham, while Yorke dropped slightly deeper to form the cutting edge of a midfield diamond. Hitzfeld's response was to introduce Mehmet Scholl in place of Alexander Zickler, as Bayern dropped, clustered and looked for quickfire counter-attacks.

Basler even attempted to bypass the slightest hint of build-up play, chancing his arm from the halfway line with an effort that only narrowly cleared Schmeichel's crossbar. Every time United pressed forward, the Germans were ready to strike back. Cole's ambitious overhead kick bounced into Kahn's midriff; Stefan Effenberg thundered one powerful effort just wide and then prompted Schmeichel to paw the ball away with an impish lob.

When the Dane was beaten, the frame of his goal contrived to help. A surging run from Basler ended with Scholl dinking a delicious chip against Schmeichel's post, before Carsten Jancker directed a close-range overhead effort against the crossbar. In between, Schmeichel also produced a full-length save from a Scholl effort that was bound for the corner.

Yet still Ferguson kept rolling the dice. Cole made way for Ole Gunnar Solskjaer and suddenly half-chances began arriving with greater regularity. The Norwegian's near-post effort forced a smart stop from Kahn, who also needed to be on his toes to keep out a glancing Solskjaer header. Still Bayern would not yield. 'I was just starting to adjust to losing the game,' admitted the United manager. 'I had reminded myself to keep my dignity and accept that it wasn't going to be our year. What then happened simply stunned me.'

When all apparent options had been exhausted, came United's wildcard: Schmeichel. Injury time was underway when the stand-in skipper sprinted forward to join the penalty area mêlée awaiting a Beckham corner. The resultant chaos disrupted the hitherto unflappable Bavarian side and Thorsten Fink's shanked clearance found only Giggs, whose equally half-hit shot was diverted past Kahn by Sheringham.

Behind the goal, United's supporters went berserk. Strangers cavorted and flares burned. From the ruins of a depressing final had risen new hope, but even that would soon make way for uncharted emotion. Bayern touched the ball just six times before it made its way to Denis Irwin, whose long pass allowed Solskjaer to win a corner.

Again Beckham swung in a delivery, but this time there would be no confusion, no scramble. Bayern

## WHAT THE PAPERS SAID

'We have never seen its like before and we will not see the like of it again. Not in our lifetimes. Not if men keep playing the world's oldest game for another 100 years and a 100 years after that. The first full century of football saved the most astonishing of all its countless dramas for the last.

'There has been nothing in the history of the people's game to compare with Manchester United's beating of not only Europe's finest but of time itself. Not the first winning of the European Cup for England by Sir Matt Busby's illustrious predecessors to last night's young champions. Not the sustained domination of football on this continent by Liverpool's majority of perfect Englishmen in the 1980s. Not the Total domination of the Dutch. And not the three successive years of technical mastery exercised by the hierarchy of last night's German opponents.

'Not even Real Madrid – much as they remain the supreme Europeans of all time – ever found themselves engaged in theatre as unbelievable as this coming to an impossible climax in front of a tumultuous gathering of 90,000 and a dumbfounded television audience of 200 million. Call it destiny, call it a miracle. Call it by whatever excess or extravagance you like. But never again describe football as only a game. Here was sporting life after seeming death. Here was glory snatched from the most unforgiving master of them all, the relentless ticking of the clock.'

Jeff Powell, *Daily Mail*

were spent. 'Sami Kuffour was marking me,' recalled Solskjaer. 'He grabbed my shirt, but then he forgot about me when the ball came over. He was busy looking at Teddy, so that was my chance to get away from him and the ball just landed on my toe.'

From there, it was prodded into the roof of the net and straight into fantasy. The Norwegian slid on his knees in celebration before disappearing under history's greatest pile-on. Supporters embodied incredulity, suspended in disbelief as they attempted to compute what had happened. When they had, droves broke down in tears of joy.

'I will always remember it for different reasons,' recalled referee Pierluigi Collina. 'First of all, the reaction of the Manchester United supporters when they scored the second goal – it was an incredible noise, like a lion's roar. Then there was the reaction of the Bayern players – their disappointment as they fell down on the pitch after conceding that goal.'

The Italian attempted to haul several Bayern players to their feet as

'The final against Bayern was, to use a cliché, a rollercoaster of emotions! For my friends and me, the build-up to the game was a two-day affair: a train to Paris, a flight to the south of France and then a hire car to Barcelona; by hook or by crook, we were going to get there! As for the game, we didn't play well and didn't offer much attacking threat, and Bayern should have been out of sight by 90 minutes. However, in all of us there was a lingering notion that it was our year, and when we equalised it was the most incredible feeling: relief, confusion and elation all rolled into one crazy moment. I was buried underneath a pile of bodies for what seemed like an eternity and when I surfaced the game had kicked off again!

'It was then that I knew we would win it. When Solskjaer scored, we were all still out of breath from celebrating the equaliser. The celebrations were amazing, strangers hugging each other and crying, everyone in a state of disbelief and euphoria. We stayed for at least an hour after the final whistle while the players took turns lifting the trophy to the crowd. I remember a reluctant Roy Keane walking through and getting the loudest cheer. I was emotionally exhausted after leaving the ground but celebrated in style and was woken by rush-hour traffic circling the roundabout I had chosen to sleep on! Without doubt, the best game of my life.'

Matt Weir, Dubai

he endeavoured to play out the final few seconds of the game. Kuffour wept and bellowed at anyone and everything, Jancker sobbed, the substituted Matthaus stared on agog from the sidelines. In a matter of moments, the turnaround was complete. The final whistle signalled some paranormal transference of energy; Bayern's players collapsed while, around them, the rejuvenated Reds sprinted and cavorted as if they could play all night.

The greatest season in the history of English football was over. The Treble was United's. 'This is the greatest moment of my life and I'm struggling to take it all in,' commented Alex Ferguson. 'I haven't said anything to my players yet. I've just hugged and kissed them. I've slobbered all over them. It was so fitting that this day would have been the ninetieth birthday of Sir Matt Busby. He will have been up there looking down on us and I think he'll have been doing a lot of kicking up there ... you can't top that; it's the pinnacle.'

A season that had eclipsed any other on all levels required a fitting climax. Though the final served up

90 minutes of largely frustrating action, those final three minutes provided a microcosm of the Treble season as a whole: whenever skill and ingenuity failed to win out, United could fall back on their sheer bloody-mindedness and refusal to accept defeat. Having rolled with the punches in the second half, Alex Ferguson's side hauled themselves up from the canvas to deliver a last-gasp one-two that will forever resound throughout football.

## THE TEAMS

**Manchester United:** Schmeichel; G.Neville, Johnsen, Stam, Irwin; Giggs, Beckham, Butt, Blomqvist (Sheringham 66); Cole (Solskjaer 80), Yorke

**Subs not used:** van der Gouw, May, P.Neville, Brown, Greening

**Goalscorers:** Sheringham 90+1, Solskjaer 90+3

**Bayern Munich:** Kahn; Linke, Matthaus (Fink 80), Kuffour; Babbel, Basler (Salihamidzic 89), Jeremies, Effenberg, Tarnat; Zickler (Scholl 71), Jancker

**Subs not used:** Dreher, Helmer, Strunz, Daei

**Goalscorer:** Basler 6

# APPENDIX

This section provides a chronological list of the 50 games that did not make it into the Top 50. There are plenty of memorable occasions in this list, but for one reason or another, they just fell short of the ones in the main section of the book. Even so, they were pretty special occasions.

MANCHESTER UNITED 8
YEOVIL TOWN 0
FA Cup fifth round
12 February 1949
Maine Road, Manchester
The giantkillers were on a roll until they met the Reds head on at Maine Road in front of over 80,000 fans. Goal-machine Jack Rowley netted five times in the club's record FA Cup triumph.

CHELSEA 5
MANCHESTER UNITED 6
Division One
16 October 1954
Stamford Bridge, London
The Busby Babes started to show their style as a splendid attacking display took the Reds to the top of the table. Dennis Viollet (three) and Tommy Taylor (two) did most of the damage.

FULHAM 3
MANCHESTER UNITED 5
FA Cup semi-final replay
26 March 1958
Highbury, London
Alex Dawson wrote himself into the record books with a hat-trick during an avalanche of goals in the capital, with Bobby Charlton fittingly scoring the late clincher a matter of weeks after the Munich disaster.

**MANCHESTER UNITED 4**
**TOTTENHAM HOTSPUR 1**
European Cup-Winners' Cup second round, second leg
10 December 1963
Old Trafford, Manchester
David Herd and Bobby Charlton shared the strikes as United superbly
overturned a two-goal deficit from the first leg. Jimmy Greaves' reply for
Spurs proved in vain.

**MANCHESTER CITY 3**
**MANCHESTER UNITED 4**
Division One
5 May 1971
Maine Road, Manchester
The final game of the season produced an explosive derby with the Trinity of
George Best (two), Bobby Charlton and Denis Law all finding the net. It meant
United finished above the Blues in the final table.

**MANCHESTER UNITED 3**
**SUNDERLAND 2**
Division Two
30 November 1974
Old Trafford, Manchester
In front of a raucous crowd of over 60,000 – the biggest in the country for
well over a year – two sides pushing for promotion produced an epic finally
settled by Willie Morgan's winner.

**MANCHESTER UNITED 2**
**DERBY COUNTY 0**
FA Cup semi-final
3 April 1976
Hillsborough, Sheffield
A brace by Gordon Hill sent United back to Wembley as the winger spanked
two long-range efforts past Graham Moseley, one from a free-kick. Tommy
Docherty's young side were good value for the win.

**MANCHESTER UNITED 2**
**LEEDS UNITED 1**
FA Cup semi-final
23 April 1977
Hillsborough, Sheffield
Leeds were beaten in their native Yorkshire as the Reds booked a return trip to
Wembley a year after losing to Southampton. Jimmy Greenhoff and Steve
Coppell scored the goals early on.

MANCHESTER UNITED 1
LIVERPOOL 0
FA Cup semi-final replay
4 April 1979
Maine Road, Manchester
Jimmy Greenhoff's header clinched a famous triumph against the league leaders and dominant force of the time, with the Reds working furiously to keep Bob Paisley's side at bay.

MANCHSTER UNITED 2
LIVERPOOL 1
Division One
5 April 1980
Old Trafford, Manchester
Things were not going to plan when Kenny Dalglish put the visitors ahead, but Mickey Thomas soon levelled. After Dalglish missed a sitter, Brian Greenhoff won it to keep United's faint title hopes alive.

MANCHESTER UNITED 5
WOLVERHAMPTON WANDERERS 0
Division One
3 October 1981
Old Trafford, Manchester
Record buy Bryan Robson signed on the pitch and then watched Sammy McIlroy bag a hat-trick, with the Reds inspired by the presence of the new arrival in the stands.

LIVERPOOL 1
MANCHESTER UNITED 2
Division One
24 October 1981
Anfield, Liverpool
Defenders Arthur Albiston and Kevin Moran were the unlikely heroes as their goals earned another splendid success against the fierce rivals from up the East Lancs Road.

ARSENAL 2
MANCHESTER UNITED 4
League Cup semi-final, first leg
15 February 1983
Highbury, London
Two-goal Steve Coppell was in red-hot form as the Gunners were 4-0 down at one stage and in danger of making the second leg an irrelevance. Norman Whiteside and Frank Stapleton also netted.

MANCHESTER UNITED 2
ARSENAL 1
FA Cup semi-final
16 April 1983
Villa Park, Birmingham
Villa Park is the happiest of hunting grounds and spectacular strikes by Bryan
Robson and Norman Whiteside propelled the Reds into the final.

MANCHESTER UNITED 4
BRIGHTON & HOVE ALBION 0
FA Cup final replay
26 May 1983
Wembley Stadium, London
After a see-saw 2-2 draw, Ron Atkinson's side lifted a first trophy in six years
in emphatic fashion, with legendary skipper Bryan Robson to the fore, scoring
twice.

MANCHESTER UNITED 1
EVERTON 0
FA Cup final
18 May 1985
Wembley Stadium, London
Down to ten men following Kevin Moran's dismissal, United overcame the
champions thanks to Norman Whiteside's exquisite extra-time curler beyond
Neville Southall.

MANCHESTER CITY 0
MANCHESTER UNITED 3
Division One
14 September 1985
Maine Road, Manchester
The Reds made an outstanding start to the campaign and the away fans inside
the ground celebrated an eighth straight win, with Bryan Robson, Arthur
Albiston and Mike Duxbury on the scoresheet.

LIVERPOOL 3
MANCHESTER UNITED 3
Division One
4 April 1988
Anfield, Liverpool
A man light and 3-1 down to England's finest, the Reds refused to be bowed
and Gordon Strachan snatched an unlikely point before a cheeky celebration
in front of the home fans.

MANCHESTER UNITED 3
LIVERPOOL 1
Division One
1 January 1989
Old Trafford, Manchester
Chinks in the Merseysiders' armour were starting to appear, as Russell Beardsmore wreaked havoc and the home crowd lapped up a pulsating performance.

MANCHESTER UNITED 4
ARSENAL 1
Division One
19 August 1989
Old Trafford, Manchester
Prospective owner Michael Knighton juggled the ball on the pitch and debutant Neil Webb volleyed a beauty as the champions succumbed in the sunshine.

NOTTINGHAM FOREST 0
MANCHESTER UNITED 1
FA Cup third round
7 January 1990
The City Ground, Nottingham
With intense pressure building on Alex Ferguson, Mark Robins came up trumps to safely negotiate the trickiest of away ties by nodding in a Mark Hughes cross.

MANCHESTER UNITED 1
CRYSTAL PALACE 0
FA Cup final replay
17 May 1990
Wembley Stadium, London
While the replay lacked the excitement of the initial 3-3 final, when Mark Hughes performed another rescue act, Lee Martin's brilliant winner ensured the first drip of what would become a torrent of trophies.

MANCHESTER UNITED 3
LIVERPOOL 1
League Cup third round
31 October 1990
Old Trafford, Manchester
Revenge was on the menu after a 4-0 defeat at Anfield a month earlier, and Steve Bruce, Mark Hughes and Lee Sharpe all struck to dump Kenny Dalglish's charges out of the cup.

**MANCHESTER UNITED 4**
**TOTTENHAM HOTSPUR 1**
Premier League
9 January 1993
Old Trafford, Manchester
Eric Cantona in his pomp was a majestic sight and he pulled the strings in this exhibition of free-flowing football. The Frenchman's pass for Denis Irwin's goal was a thing of beauty.

**MANCHESTER UNITED 5**
**SHEFFIELD WEDNESDAY 0**
Premier League
16 March 1994
Old Trafford, Manchester
Four goals inside 45 one-sided minutes illustrated the power and panache of Alex Ferguson's top dogs. Eric Cantona added his second goal after the break, but it could have been much worse for the outclassed Owls.

**MANCHESTER UNITED 4**
**OLDHAM ATHLETIC 1**
FA Cup semi-final replay
13 April 1994
Maine Road, Manchester
Mark Hughes' Wembley thunderbolt had rescued United's Double hopes, and a rampant replay display was capped by goals from Denis Irwin, Andrei Kanchelskis, Bryan Robson and Ryan Giggs.

**BLACKBURN ROVERS 1**
**MANCHESTER UNITED 2**
Premier League
28 August 1995
Ewood Park, Blackburn
United's youngsters came of age to upset the champions and lay the marker for a second Double triumph. Lee Sharpe and David Beckham were on the mark as Rovers suffered an early-season reverse.

**LIVERPOOL 1**
**MANCHESTER UNITED 3**
Premier League
19 April 1997
Anfield, Liverpool
'We won the Football League again, this time on Merseyside' crowed the away end as Andy Cole capitalised on a David James error to wrap up the sweetest of successes after a Gary Pallister brace.

MANCHESTER UNITED 3
FC BARCELONA 3
Champions League group stage
16 September 1998
Old Trafford, Manchester
Goals galore seemed guaranteed when these two superpowers locked horns and a thrilling tie unfolded. David Beckham's free-kick was one of the highlights.

MANCHESTER UNITED 2
INTER MILAN 0
Champions League quarter-final, first leg
3 March 1999
Old Trafford, Manchester
Dwight Yorke was emerging as one of the best strikers in Europe and his headed double accounted for Inter on a memorable night, although Peter Schmeichel also had to be at his best.

CHELSEA 0
MANCHESTER UNITED 2
FA Cup quarter-final replay
10 March 1999
Stamford Bridge, London
Many had written off United's hopes ahead of this replay, but an under-strength side silenced Stamford Bridge with Dwight Yorke at the double.

MANCHESTER UNITED 1
PALMEIRAS 0
Intercontinental Cup
30 November 1999
Tokyo National Stadium
The Treble winners became Britain's first-ever world champions thanks to skipper Roy Keane's effort, but Mark Bosnich and Ryan Giggs were the stars on the day.

MANCHESTER UNITED 7
WEST HAM UNITED 1
Premier League
1 April 2000
Old Trafford, Manchester
Craig Forrest let in nine in his Ipswich days and was on the wrong end of another battering, with Paul Scholes hitting a treble after United fell behind early on.

ASTON VILLA 2
MANCHESTER UNITED 3
FA Cup third round
6 January 2002
Villa Park, Birmingham
Trailing 2-0 and facing elimination at the first hurdle, the Reds rallied and
substitute Ruud van Nistelrooy's two goals in two minutes past Peter
Schmeichel sparked a jubilant pitch invasion.

JUVENTUS 0
MANCHESTER UNITED 3
Champions League phase two
25 February 2003
Stadio delle Alpi, Turin
It's difficult to imagine Ryan Giggs prompting fan discontent, but he answered
any critics with a dramatic introduction as substitute, scoring twice (including
a superb solo effort), before going off on 48 minutes.

EVERTON 3
MANCHESTER UNITED 4
Premier League
7 February 2004
Goodison Park, Liverpool
The Toffees battled back from a 3-0 half-time deficit to stun Sir Alex's side
but, somehow, the Reds mustered one last response late on, with Ruud van
Nistelrooy heading home Cristiano Ronaldo's cross.

MANCHESTER UNITED 1
ARSENAL 0
FA Cup semi-final
3 April 2004
Villa Park, Birmingham
'United's fans refused to even consider defeat,' said one newspaper report, as
the Reds were roared to a hard-fought win courtesy of Paul Scholes' solitary
strike.

MANCHESTER UNITED 6
FENERBAHCE 2
Champions League group stages
28 September 2004
Old Trafford, Manchester
As debuts go, this was surely one of the best ever. Wayne Rooney introduced
himself to the Old Trafford faithful with a blistering hat-trick on the European
stage.

MANCHESTER UNITED 2
ARSENAL 0
Premier League
24 October 2004
Old Trafford, Manchester
A match known for 'Pizzagate' and the end of the Gunners' 49-match
unbeaten streak – a damaging defeat that Arsène Wenger's champions did not
take too well.

LIVERPOOL 0
MANCHESTER UNITED 1
Premier League
3 March 2007
Anfield, Liverpool
In front of the Kop end, in the last minute of a game Liverpool had largely
controlled, John O'Shea pounced when Pepe Reina parried a Cristiano Ronaldo
free-kick.

MANCHESTER UNITED 3
AC MILAN 2
Champions League semi-final, first leg
24 April 2007
Old Trafford, Manchester
On a night when some big names enhanced their reputations, Wayne Rooney's
late drive gave United a lead to take to Italy. Cristiano Ronaldo and Rooney
shone but, unfortunately, so did Kaka for the visitors.

MANCHESTER UNITED 6
NEWCASTLE UNITED 0
Premier League
12 January 2008
Old Trafford, Manchester
Cristiano Ronaldo's only hat-trick in United colours provided the backbone of
a one-sided mauling of the Magpies, with only Shay Given preventing an
embarrassment.

MANCHESTER UNITED 4
ARSENAL 0
FA Cup fifth round
16 February 2008
Old Trafford, Manchester
An unorthodox line-up had the fans puzzled, but a remarkable dismantling of
the Gunners punctured their confidence and struck a huge psychological blow.

WIGAN ATHLETIC 0
MANCHESTER UNITED 2
Premier League
11 May 2008
The JJB Stadium, Wigan
Cristiano Ronaldo's penalty was edging United to the title on the last day, but Ryan Giggs came off the bench to equal Sir Bobby Charlton's appearance record and ease the tension late on.

MANCHESTER UNITED 1
LIGA DE QUITO 0
Club World Cup final
21 December 2008
International Stadium, Yokohama
Wayne Rooney confirmed United's status as the world's best side with the only goal in front of a sell-out crowd, after Nemanja Vidic was sent off at the start of the second half.

MANCHESTER UNITED 5
TOTTENHAM HOTSPUR 2
Premier League
25 April 2009
Old Trafford, Manchester
United never accept defeat against Spurs and scored five times in the second half after coming out for the restart 2-0 down to keep the title bid on track.

MANCHESTER UNITED 3
MANCHESTER CITY 1
League Cup semi-final, second leg
27 January 2010
Old Trafford, Manchester
The noisy neighbours were dreaming of Wembley after the first-leg win, but United dominated and Wayne Rooney's late header brought the house down.

MANCHESTER UNITED 4
AC MILAN 0
Champions League round of 16
10 March 2010
Old Trafford, Manchester
A genuine humbling of the Rossoneri's old guard and the chance for the Theatre of Dreams to welcome David Beckham back to the club he served with distinction.

MANCHESTER UNITED 3
LIVERPOOL 2
Premier League
19 September 2010
Old Trafford, Manchester
Dimitar Berbatov was the toast of Old Trafford after a memorable hat-trick
silenced the dogged Merseysiders, with a sensational overhead kick the pick of
the bunch.

WEST HAM UNITED 2
MANCHESTER UNITED 4
Premier League
2 April 2011
Upton Park, London
Behind to two penalties, another championship surge looked like being
derailed, only for Wayne Rooney to smash a hat-trick and Javier Hernandez
added the *coup de grâce*.

# PICTURE CREDITS

## SECTION 1

Page 1: Action Images, Getty Images, Manchester United, Getty Images
Page 2: Action Images, Getty Images, Getty Images, Getty Images
Page 3: Manchester United, Manchester United, Getty Images, Getty Images
Page 4: Getty Images, Getty Images, Mirrorpix
Page 5: Getty Images, Getty Images, Getty Images
Page 6: Getty Images, Getty Images, Getty Images
Page 7: Getty Images, Getty Images, Getty Images
Page 8: Manchester United, Getty Images, Getty Images

## SECTION 2

Page 9: Manchester United, Getty Images, Manchester United
Page 10: Manchester United, Getty Images, Mirrorpix
Page 11: Manchester United, Manchester United, Getty Images
Page 12: Mirrorpix, Manchester United, Getty Images
Page 13: Manchester United, Getty Images, Getty Images
Page 14: Action Images, Getty Images, Getty Images
Page 15: Getty Images, Getty Images, Manchester United
Page 16: Manchester United, Getty Images